RICE & GRAINS

THE BEST-EVER STEP-BY-STEP RECIPE BOOK

RICE & GRAINS

THE BEST-EVER STEP-BY-STEP RECIPE BOOK

85 sensational high-fibre, low-GI recipes in 400 colour photographs

**Supercharge your diet with nutritious rice, oats, wheat,
barley, rye, corn and quinoa**

Editor: Rosie Gordon

southwater

This edition is published by Southwater, an imprint of Anness Publishing Ltd, Hermes House, 88–89 Blackfriars Road, London SE1 8HA; tel. 020 7401 2077; fax 020 7633 9499 www.southwaterbooks.com; www.annesspublishing.com

If you like the images in this book and would like to investigate using them for publishing, promotions or advertising, please visit our website www.practicalpictures.com for more information.

UK agent: The Manning Partnership Ltd; tel. 01225 478444; fax 01225 478440; sales@manning-partnership.co.uk
UK distributor: Grantham Book Services Ltd; tel. 01476 541080; fax 01476 541061; orders@gbs.tbs-ltd.co.uk
North American agent/distributor: National Book Network; tel. 301 459 3366; fax 301 429 5746; www.nbnbooks.com
Australian agent/distributor: Pan Macmillan Australia; tel. 1300 135 113; fax 1300 135 103; customer.service@macmillan.com.au
New Zealand agent/distributor: David Bateman Ltd; tel. (09) 415 7664; fax (09) 415 8892

Publisher: Joanna Lorenz
Editorial Director: Helen Sudell
Editor: Rosie Gordon
Designers: Diane Pullen and Ian Sandom
Production Controller: Steve Lang

ETHICAL TRADING POLICY
Because of our ongoing ecological investment programme, you, as our customer, can have the pleasure and reassurance of knowing that a tree is being cultivated on your behalf to naturally replace the materials used to make the book you are holding. For further information about this scheme, go to www.annesspublishing.com/trees

© Anness Publishing Ltd 2008

A CIP catalogue record for this book is available from the British Library.

Previously published as part of a larger volume, *Cooking with Beans, Grains, Pulses and Legumes* by Nicola Graimes.

NOTES

Bracketed terms are for American readers.

For all recipes, quantities are given in both metric and imperial measures and, where appropriate, in standard cups and spoons. Follow one set of measures, but not a mixture, because they are not interchangeable.

Standard spoon and cup measures are level. 1 tsp = 5ml, 1 tbsp = 15ml, 1 cup = 250ml/8fl oz.

Australian standard tablespoons are 20ml. Australian readers should use 3 tsp in place of 1 tbsp for measuring small quantities of gelatine, flour, salt, etc.

The nutritional analysis given for each recipe is calculated per portion (i.e. serving or item), unless otherwise stated. If the recipe gives a range, such as Serves 4–6, then the nutritional analysis will be for the smaller portion size, i.e. 6 servings. Measurements for sodium do not include salt added to taste.

Medium (US large) eggs are used unless otherwise stated.

CONTENTS

INTRODUCTION

For thousands of years, rice and other cereal grains have been staple foods for many civilizations. Climate and growing conditions have influenced the enduring popularity of certain types throughout the world: wheat, barley, oats and rye prevail in Europe; corn in America; buckwheat in Russia and Central Asia; quinoa in South America; rice in the Far East; and sorghum and millet in Africa. While the consumption of grains in the form of bread and pasta is very prevalent in the West, in the East noodles and rice form a large part of the daily diet.

Rice is the world's largest crop, followed by corn and wheat. About 2 billion people rely on rice as their primary food every day. Rice farming is well suited to countries and regions with low labour costs and high rainfall, as it is very labour-intensive to farm and requires plenty of water for irrigation. Although rice is native to South Asia and certain parts of Africa, it is increasingly eaten in many other regions, particularly with the fashion for Asian cuisines.

VERSATILITY

What is truly remarkable about grains is their versatility and how they have been transformed throughout the world into a staggering range of foods. They are experiencing a resurgence in popularity, and have become "upwardly mobile" – wholegrains are no longer seen as a poor man's food or that of the puritanical health fanatic. With this renewed interest, we've seen new, or more accurately, previously unseen, grain varieties on many restaurant menus and in food shops. Spelt, quinoa, polenta, soba and freekah are increasingly fashionable.

Moreover, grains can be used in many different dishes, as the textures vary in the way they are cooked to work

Above: Oat cakes make a satisfying snack that is high in fibre and low in fat. Crunchy seeds give extra flavour.

well with sweet or creamy dishes, powerful spices or mellow, savoury flavours alike.

HEALTH ATTRIBUTES

Grains contain a high concentration of nutrients, considering their size. Whole grains contain a balance of carbohydrates, protein, fat and vitamins and minerals, and are healthier when unrefined. When processed or refined, as in white flour, much of the fibre, B vitamins, vitamin E, iron and other trace minerals are lost. Most grains can be sprouted, which greatly enhances their nutritional value.

Recently, scientists at University College, London discovered that a diet rich in beans, nuts and cereals could be a way to help prevent cancer. They found that these foods contain a potent anti-cancer compound, which, researchers say, in the future may be possible to mimic in an anti-cancer drug.

Grains are largely made up of carbohydrates, from about 65 to 90 per cent of the calorie content, depending on the variety of grain. Protein usually accounts for 7 to 15 per cent of the calories and the fat contained within the

Left: Rye bread is more dense than wheat bread as it lacks gluten. It is also higher in fibre.

Above: Grains are important as part of a balanced diet. Here, rice noodles are combined with spiced chicken and wrapped in lettuce leaves.

germ makes up the remainder. Grains do not contain any of the saturated fat or cholesterol that are often linked to health problems such as heart disease.

Whole grains are a good source of vitamins and minerals, especially in the bran and germ. Insoluble fibre in the bran is important for a healthy digestive system and bowel, and soluble fibre helps to lower the cholesterol level in the blood. Unrefined or whole grains tend to have a low glycaemic index, which means they are digested slowly,

Below: Polenta is a versatile grain and is available in different forms.

allowing you to feel full for longer and keep your glucose levels under control. This may help people to avoid late-onset diabetes, among other health complaints. When grains and grain products (especially whole grains and whole grain products) are part of a balanced diet, including fruit and vegetables, pulses and dairy products, as well as meat and fish, they are one of the most important foods for providing proper nutrition.

Certain grains have been found to be particularly nutritious. For example, the UN has classified quinoa as a supercrop because of its exceptionally high protein count and balanced set of essential amino acids, which make it an unusually complete food.

Rice is cholesterol and fat-free, sodium-free, a complex carbohydrate, gluten-free and non-allergenic. It is also easy to digest. Get to know the different types available – for example, basmati rice has a far lower GI than jasmine rice. This book guides you through the many varieties you will find in the shops today. Rice is often the grain of choice for people who have developed a wheat or gluten intolerance.

Recently it has become easy to find flours made from rice, millet and many other grains in the supermarket, so that you can make your own pasta, bread and

Below: Noodles are a staple food for many cultures. The many varieties include wheat, rice and egg noodles.

cakes that use a good variety of grains. Also, health stores stock grain flakes of many varieties so that you can invent your own breakfast cereals.

STORAGE
One of the greatest advantages of grains is that they have a long shelf life if stored in dry, cool, airtight containers away from sunlight. Some whole grains can be kept without any damage or loss of nutritional value for up to two years, although flaked and cracked grains and flour should be used within 2–3 months of purchase.

ABOUT THIS BOOK
As well as a discussion of the various types of rice and grain available, this book gives you 85 recipes that will begin to widen your repertoire of grain foods. Swap your usual bowl of cereal or sandwich for more exciting alternatives, including fruity smoothies for breakfast, filling soups and salads, risottos, bakes, delicious desserts and more, with something to suit all occasions, from packed lunches to dinner parties.

CEREAL
The word cereal has its origin in the name of the Roman goddess of grain, Ceres. Grains, otherwise known as cereals, are the edible seeds of plants, usually members of the grass family, although there are exceptions. They are annuals that have to be planted every year. Cereals are grown in huge quantities all around the world, and provide more food energy to the human race than any other crop. Grains are highly nutritious, especially when unrefined.

RICE

Throughout Asia, a meal is considered incomplete without rice. It is a staple food for over half the world's population, and almost every culture has its own repertoire of rice dishes, ranging from risottos to pilaffs. What's more, this valuable food provides a good source of vitamins and minerals, as well as a steady supply of energy.

Below and right: Brown and white long grain rice.

Below: Jasmine fragrant rice.

Long Grain Rice

The most widely used type of rice is long grain rice, where the grain is five times as long as it is wide. Long grain brown rice has had its outer husk removed, leaving the bran and germ intact, which gives it a chewy, nutty flavour. It takes longer to cook than white rice but contains more fibre, vitamins and minerals. Long grain white rice has had its husk, bran and germ removed, taking most of the nutrients with them and leaving a mild-tasting rice that is light and fluffy when cooked. It is often whitened with chalk, talc or other preservatives, so rinsing is essential. Easy-cook long grain white rice, sometimes called parboiled or converted rice, has been steamed under pressure. This process hardens the grain and makes it difficult to overcook, and some nutrients are transferred from the bran and germ into the kernel during this process. Easy-cook brown rice cooks more quickly than normal brown rice.

Jasmine Rice

This rice has a soft, sticky texture and a delicious, mildly perfumed flavour – which accounts for its other name, fragrant rice. It is a long grain rice that is widely used in Thai cooking, where its delicate flavour tempers strongly spiced food.

COOKING LONG GRAIN BROWN RICE

There are many methods and opinions on how to cook perfect, light fluffy rice. The absorption method is one of the simplest and retains valuable nutrients, which would otherwise be lost in cooking water that is drained away.

Different types of rice have different powers of absorption. However, the general rule of thumb for long grain rice is to use double the volume of water to rice. For example, use 1 cup of rice to 2 cups of water. 200g/7oz/1 cup long grain rice is sufficient to feed about four people as a side dish.

1 Rinse the rice in a sieve (strainer) under cold, running water. Place in a heavy pan and add the measured cold water. Bring to the boil, uncovered, then reduce the heat and stir the rice. Add salt, to taste, if you wish.

2 Cover the pan. Simmer over a very low heat for 25–35 minutes, without removing the lid, until the water is absorbed and the rice tender. Remove from the heat and leave to stand, covered, for 5 minutes before serving.

Basmati Rice

This is a slender, long grain rice, which is grown in the foothills of the Himalayas. It is aged for a year after harvest, giving it a characteristic light, fluffy texture and aromatic flavour. Its name means "fragrant".

White and brown types of basmati rice are available. Brown basmati contains more nutrients, and has a slightly nuttier flavour than the white variety. Widely used in Indian cooking, basmati rice has a cooling effect on hot and spicy curries. It is also excellent for biryanis and for rice salads, when you want very light, fluffy separate grains.

Red Rice

This rice comes from the Camargue in France and has a distinctive chewy texture and a nutty flavour. It is an unusually hard grain, which although it takes almost an hour to cook, retains its shape. Cooking intensifies its red colour, making it a distinctive addition to salads and stuffings.

Wild Rice

This is not a true rice but an aquatic grass grown in North America. It has dramatic, long, slender brown-black grains that have a nutty flavour and chewy texture. It takes longer to cook than most types of rice – from 35–60 minutes, depending on whether you like it chewy or tender – but you can reduce the cooking time by soaking it in water overnight. Wild rice is extremely nutritious. It contains all eight essential amino acids and is particularly rich in lysine. It is a good source of fibre, low in calories and gluten free. Use in stuffings, serve plain or mix with other rices in pilaffs and rice salads.

QUICK WAYS TO FLAVOUR RICE

• Cook brown rice in vegetable stock with sliced dried apricots. Sauté an onion in a little oil and add ground cumin, coriander and fresh chopped chilli, then mix in the cooked rice.

• Add raisins and toasted almonds to saffron-infused rice.

Above: Red rice.

Above: Wild rice.

Above: White and brown basmati rice.

Right:
Calasparra rice.

Calasparra Rice

Traditionally used for making Spanish paella, this short grain rice is not as sturdy as risotto rice and needs to be handled with care because it breaks down easily. The best way of cooking paella is to leave the rice unstirred once all the ingredients have been added to the pan.

Risotto Rice

To make Italian risotto, it is essential that you use a special, fat, short grain rice. Arborio rice, which originates from the Po Valley region in Italy, is the most widely sold variety of risotto rice, but you may also find varieties such as carnaroli and vialone nano. It is best to add the cooking liquid gradually and allow it to be absorbed before adding the next ladleful. When cooked, most rice absorbs around three times its weight in water, but risotto rice can absorb nearly five times its weight, and the result is a creamy grain that retains a slight bite.

QUICK WAYS TO FLAVOUR RISOTTO

• When making risotto, replace a quarter of the vegetable stock with red or white wine.

• Add a bay leaf, the juice and rind of a lemon, or a lemon grass stalk, and cardamom pods to the cooking water.

• Saffron adds a yellow colour to risotto rice. Add a few threads to the vegetable stock.

Above: Clockwise from left: arbo-
rio, carnaroli and vialone nano
risotto rice.

MAKING A SIMPLE RISOTTO

A good risotto – creamy and moist with tender grains that retain a slight bite – is easy to make. The secrets are to use the correct type of rice (arborio, carnaroli, or vialone nano); to add the cooking liquid gradually – it should be completely absorbed by the rice before the next ladleful is added; and to stir the risotto frequently to prevent the grains from sticking to the pan.

SERVES FOUR

INGREDIENTS
  15ml/1 tbsp olive oil
  small knob (pat) of butter
  1 onion, finely chopped
  350g/12oz/1¾ cups risotto rice
  1.2 litres/2 pints stock, simmering
  50g/2oz/⅔ cup freshly grated
    Parmesan cheese
  salt and ground black pepper

VARIATIONS
• Add finely chopped cooked (not pickled) beetroot towards the end of cooking to give the rice a vibrant pink colour and slight sweetness.
• To make mushroom and broccoli risotto, sauté 175g/6oz/2 cups sliced flat mushrooms with the onion. Blanch 225g/8oz/2 cups broccoli florets for 3 minutes until tender, and add towards the end of cooking time.

1 Heat the oil and butter in a large, heavy pan, then cook the onion for 7 minutes until soft, stirring occasionally. Add the rice and stir to coat the grains in the hot oil and butter.

2 Add a quarter of the stock and cook over a low-medium heat, stirring until the liquid is absorbed. Add more stock, a little at a time, stirring, until all the liquid is added and absorbed.

3 After about 20 minutes, the grains will be creamy but still retain a bite. Turn off the heat, stir in the Parmesan and check the seasoning. Add salt and pepper to taste and serve immediately.

JAPANESE RICE PRODUCTS

The Japanese are very resourceful when it comes to exploiting the vast potential of rice.

Sake: This spirit is Japan's national drink and comes in various grades. It can be used in cooking, especially to tenderize meat.

Mirin: Sweet rice wine that is delicious in marinades and savoury dishes, and is a key ingredient in teriyaki.

Rice vinegar: Popular throughout Asia, this ranges in colour from white to brown. Japanese rice vinegar has a mild, mellow flavour. The Chinese version is much harsher.

Amasake: A healthful rice drink made by adding enzymes from fermented rice to wholegrain pudding rice. It has a similar consistency to soya "milk" and can be flavoured. Amasake can be used for baking or to make creamy desserts. It is also an excellent and easily digestible weaning food.

Above: Clockwise from top left: Amasake, mirin, rice vinegar and sake.

Pudding Rice

This rounded, short grain rice is suitable for milk puddings and rice desserts. The grains swell and absorb a great deal of milk during cooking, which gives the pudding a soft, creamy consistency. Brown pudding rice is also available.

Glutinous Rice

This rice is almost round in shape and has a slightly sweet flavour. Despite its name, the rice is gluten-free. The grains stick together when cooked due to their high starch content, making the rice easier to eat with chopsticks. Glutinous rice, which can be either white, black or purple, is used in many South-east Asian countries to make sticky, creamy puddings. In China, white glutinous rice is often wrapped in lotus leaves and steamed to make a popular dim sum dish.

Right: White and black glutinous rice.

Left: Pudding rice.

Japanese Sushi Rice

Similar to glutinous rice, this is mixed with a rice vinegar dressing to make sushi. Most sushi rice eaten in the West is grown in California.

Buying and Storing Rice: To ensure freshness, always buy rice from shops that have a regular turnover of stock. Store in an airtight container in a cool, dry, dark place to keep out moisture and insects. Wash before use to remove any impurities. Cooked rice should be cooled quickly, then chilled and reheated thoroughly before serving.

Health Benefits of Rice: Rice is a source of complex carbohydrates and fibre. In its whole form it is a good source of B vitamins. White rice is deprived of much of its nutrients because the bran and germ have been removed. The starch in brown rice is absorbed slowly, keeping blood sugar levels even and making it a useful food for diabetics. Research shows that rice may benefit sufferers of psoriasis. It can also be used to treat digestive disorders, calm the nervous system, prevent kidney stones and reduce the risk of bowel cancer. However, the phytates in brown rice can inhibit the absorption of iron and calcium.

Above: Sushi rice.

QUICK IDEAS FOR RICE
Rice can be served plain, but it is also good in one-dish meals, marrying well with a host of exotic flavourings and simple store-cupboard ingredients.

• To make a Middle-Eastern inspired rice dish, cook long grain brown rice in vegetable stock, then stir in some toasted flaked almonds, chopped dried dates and figs, thoroughly rinsed canned chickpeas, and chopped fresh mint.

• For a simple pilao, gently fry a finely chopped onion in sunflower oil with cardamom pods, a cinnamon stick and cloves, then stir in basmati rice. Add water, infused with a pinch of saffron, and cook until tender. Towards the end of the cooking time, add sultanas (golden raisins) and cashew nuts, then garnish with fresh coriander (cilantro). This is good with grilled meat.

RICE PRODUCTS
Rice flakes: These are made by steaming and rolling whole or white grains. They are light and quick-cooking, and can be added raw to muesli or used to make porridge, creamy puddings, bread, biscuits and cakes.

Rice bran: Like wheat and oat bran, rice bran comes from the husk of the grain kernel. It is high in soluble fibre and useful for adding texture and substance to bread, cakes and biscuits, and stews.

Rice flour: Often used to make sticky Asian cakes and sweets, rice flour can also be used to thicken sauces. Because rice flour does not contain gluten, cakes made with it are rather flat. It can be combined with wheat flour to make cakes and bread, but produces a crumbly loaf. Rice powder is a very fine rice flour, found in Asian shops.

Right: Clockwise from top left: rice bran, rice flour, rice powder and rice flakes.

WHEAT GRAINS

By far the most popular grain in Europe and North America, where if grows well, wheat is a highly versatile cereal. Its texture and high gluten content make it ideal for grinding and making into bread, cakes and other baked foods, as well as the ever popular pasta. As it is inexpensive, readily available and nutritious, wheat should form a major part in our diet. Of course, many of the bought goods associated with it are fatty or high in sugar, but you can easily make your own, healthier treats.

WHEAT

The largest and most important grain crop in the world, there are said to be more than 30,000 varieties of wheat. Present day wheat varieties are believed to have derived from a hybrid wild wheat that grew in the Middle East about 10,000 years ago. The wheat kernel comprises three parts: bran, germ and endosperm. Wheat bran is the outer husk, while wheat germ is the nutritious seed from which the plant grows.

Sprouted wheat is an excellent food, often recommended in cancer-prevention diets. The endosperm, the inner part of the kernel, is full of starch and protein, and forms the basis of wheat flour. In addition to flour, wheat comes in various other forms.

Wheat Berries

These are whole wheat grains with the husks removed and they can be bought in health food shops. Wheat berries may be used to add a sweet, nutty flavour and chewy texture to breads, soups and stews, or can be combined with rice or other grains. Wheat berries must be soaked overnight, then cooked in boiling water until tender. If they are left to germinate, the berries sprout into wheatgrass, a powerful detoxifier and cleanser (see below).

Wheat Bran

The outer husk of the wheat kernel is known as wheatbran and is a by-product of white flour production. It is very high in insoluble dietary fibre, which absorbs water and promotes healthy bowel activity. Wheat bran makes a healthy addition to bread doughs, breakfast cereals, cakes, muffins and biscuits (cookies), and it can be used to add substance to stews and bakes.

Above: Wholewheat berries.

Below: Wheatgrass.

WHEATGRASS – A NATURAL HEALER

Grown from the whole wheat grain, wheatgrass has been recognized for centuries for its general healing qualities. When juiced, it is a powerful detoxifier and cleanser and is a rich source of B vitamins and vitamins A, C and E, as well as the many minerals and phyto-nutrients. It is also a complete source of protein. Its vibrant green colour comes from chlorophyll (known as "nature's healer"), which works directly on the liver to eliminate harmful toxins. It is also reputed to have anti-ageing capabilities. Once it is juiced, wheatgrass must be consumed within 15 minutes, preferably on an empty stomach. Some people may experience nausea or dizziness when drinking the juice for the first time, but this will soon pass.

Wheat Flakes

Steamed and softened berries that have been rolled and pressed are known as wheat flakes or rolled wheat. They are best used on their own or mixed with other flaked grains in porridge, as a base for muesli, or to add nutrients and substance to breads and cakes.

Wheat Germ

The nutritious heart of the whole wheat berry, wheat germ is a rich source of protein, vitamins B and E, and iron. It is used in much the same way as wheat bran and lends a pleasant, nutty flavour to breakfast cereals and porridge. Wheat germ is available toasted or untoasted. Store it in an airtight container in the refrigerator as it can become rancid if kept at room temperature.

Cracked Wheat

This is made from crushed wheat berries and retains all the nutrients of whole-wheat. Often confused with bulgur wheat, cracked wheat can be used in the same way as wheat berries (although it cooks in less time), or as an alternative to rice and other grains. When cooked, it has a slightly sticky texture and pleasant crunchiness. Serve it as a side dish or use in salads and pilaffs.

Bulgur Wheat

Unlike cracked wheat, this grain is made from cooked wheat berries with the bran removed, and then dried and crushed. This light, nutty grain is simply soaked in water for 20 minutes, then drained – some manufacturers specify cold water but boiling water produces a softer grain. It can also be cooked in boiling water until tender. Bulgur wheat is the main ingredient in the Middle Eastern salad, tabbouleh, where it is combined with chopped parsley, mint, tomatoes, cucumber and onion, and dressed with lemon juice and olive oil. It can also be used as an alternative to couscous.

Right: Wheat germ.

Right: Wheat flakes.

Right: Bulgur wheat.

COOKING WHEAT BERRIES

Wheat berries make a delicious addition to salads, and they can also be used to add a pleasant texture to breads and stews.

1 Place the wheat berries in a bowl and cover with cold water. Soak overnight, then rinse thoroughly and drain well.

2 Place the wheat berries in a pan with water. Bring to the boil, then cover and simmer for 1–2 hours until tender, replenishing the water when necessary.

Semolina

Made from the endosperm of durum wheat, semolina can be used to make a hot milk pudding or it can be added to cakes, biscuits and breads to give them a pleasant grainy texture.

Couscous

Although it looks like a grain, couscous consists of coarsely ground wheat semolina. It can also be made with corn, millet, freekah or sorghum. Couscous is popular in North Africa, where it forms

Above: Semolina.

COOKING COUSCOUS

Traditionally, the preparation of couscous is a time-consuming business, requiring lengthy steaming. The couscous found in most shops nowadays, however, is precooked, which cuts the preparation time drastically.

1 Place the couscous in a large bowl, add enough boiling water to cover and leave for 10 minutes or until all the water has been absorbed. Separate the grains, season and mix in a knob of butter.

2 Alternatively, moisten the grains and place in a muslin-lined steamer. Steam for 15 minutes or until the grains are tender and fluffy.

the basis of a national dish of the same name. Individual grains are moistened by hand, passed through a sieve and then steamed in a couscousière, suspended over a bubbling vegetable stew, until light and fluffy. Nowadays, the couscous that is generally available is the instant variety, which simply needs soaking in boiling water, although it can also be steamed or baked. Couscous has a fairly bland flavour, which makes it a good foil for spicy dishes.

Wheat Flour

This is ground from the whole grain and may be wholemeal (whole-wheat), brown or white, depending on the degree of processing. Hard, or strong flour is high in a protein called gluten, which makes it ideal for bread making, while soft flour is lower in gluten but higher in starch and is better for light cakes and pastries. Durum wheat flour comes from one of the hardest varieties of wheat and is used to make pasta. Most commercial white flour is a combination of soft and hard wheat, which produces an "all-purpose" flour.

Since the refining process robs many flours (white and lower extraction-rate types) of most of their nutrients, the lost vitamins and minerals are replaced with supplements. Unbleached and organically produced flours have fewer chemical additives. Nutritionally, stone-ground wholemeal or whole-wheat flour is the best buy because it is largely unprocessed and retains all the valuable nutrients. It produces slightly heavier breads, cakes and pastries than white flour, but can be combined with white flour to make lighter versions, although, of course, the nutritional value will not be as high.

Farro

This is another type of ancient wheat that is becoming increasingly favoured. It is grown in certain parts of Italy, where it is turned into various forms, including whole, pearled, cracked or flour. Farro can be used in soups, or to make risottos or pilaffs.

Freekah

Pronounced "freeka", this traditional grain is processed from durum wheat and harvested while young and green. The grains are then roasted and dried. It has a crunchy texture and is a good alternative to rice. Freekah has a low glycaemic index (GI) and four times the fibre of brown rice. It also has a high protein content and is rich in iron, zinc and calcium. As with the other traditional forms of wheat, freekah is said to be tolerated by those with wheat allergy.

Kamut

An ancient relative of durum wheat, this grain has long, large, brown kernels with a creamy, nutty flavour. It is as versatile as wheat and, when ground into flour, can be used to make pasta, breads, cakes and pastry. Puffed kamut cereals

Above: Couscous.

SEITAN

Used as a meat replacement, seitan is made from wheat gluten and has a firm, chewy texture. It can be found in the chiller cabinet of health food shops. Seitan has a neutral flavour that benefits from marinating. Slice or cut into chunks and stir-fry, or add to stews and pasta sauces during the last few minutes of cooking time. Seitan does not need to be cooked for long, just heated through.

*Wheat flour (below)
and malted brown
flour, which contains
flour from malted
wheat grains.
Stoneground versions
are available.*

and kamut crackers are available in health food shops. Kamut has a higher nutritional value than wheat and is easier to digest. Although it contains gluten, people suffering from coeliac disease have found that they can tolerate the grain if eaten in moderation.

Spelt

This is one of the most ancient cultivated wheats and, because of its high nutritional value, is becoming more widely available. Spelt grain looks very similar to wheat and the flour can be substituted for wheat flour in bread. However, it is richer in vitamins and minerals than wheat, and in a more readily digestible form. Although spelt contains

gluten, it usually can be tolerated in moderate amounts by people suffering from coeliac disease.

Buying and Storing Wheat Grains: Buy wheat-based foods from shops with a high turnover of stock. Wheat berries can be kept for around 6 months, but wholewheat flour should be used within 3 months, as its oils turn rancid. Always decant grains into airtight containers and store in a cool, dark place. Wheat germ deteriorates very quickly at room temperature and should be stored in an airtight container in the refrigerator for no more than a month.

Health Benefits of Wheat Grains: Wheat is most nutritious when it is unprocessed and in its whole form. (When milled into

> ### COELIAC DISEASE
> This is caused by a reaction to gluten, a substance found in some cereals. It is estimated that thousands of people suffer from the disease, many without diagnosis. Symptoms may include anaemia, weight loss, fatigue, depression and diarrhoea. Wheat, rye, barley and sometimes oats are the main culprits and sufferers are usually advised to remove these completely from their diet. Rice, soya, buckwheat, quinoa, millet and corn are gluten-free substitutes.

white flour, wheat loses a staggering 80 per cent of its nutrients.) Wheat is an excellent source of dietary fibre, the B vitamins and vitamin E, as well as iron, selenium and zinc. Fibre is the most discussed virtue of whole wheat and most of this is concentrated in the bran. Eating one or more spoonfuls of bran a day is recommended to relieve constipation. Numerous studies show fibre to be effective in inhibiting colon and rectal cancer, varicose veins, haemorrhoids and obesity. Additionally, phytoestrogens found in whole grains may ward off breast cancer. On the negative side, wheat is also a well-known allergen and triggers coeliac disease, a gluten intolerance, although varieties of wheat, such as spelt and kamut, have been found to be tolerated by some coeliacs if eaten in moderation.

Left: Seitan.

OTHER GRAINS

WHEAT AND RICE ARE THE MOST FAMILIAR AND WIDELY USED GRAINS, BUT DON'T FORGET THE WEALTH OF OTHER GRAINS THAT ARE AVAILABLE, INCLUDING OATS, RYE, CORN, QUINOA AND BARLEY.

OATS

Available whole, rolled, flaked, as oatmeal or oatbran, oats are warming and sustaining when cooked. Like rye, oats are popular in northern Europe, particularly Scotland. They are commonly turned into porridge, oatcakes and pancakes, and used raw in muesli.

Whole oats are unprocessed with the nutritious bran and germ remaining intact. Oat groats are the hulled, whole kernel, while rolled oats are made from groats that have been heated and pressed flat. Quick-cooking rolled oats have been pre-cooked in water and then dried, which diminishes their nutritional value. Medium oatmeal is best in cakes and breads, while fine is ideal in pancakes, and fruit and milk drinks. Oatmeal and oat flour contain very little gluten so should be mixed with wheat flour to make leavened bread. Oat bran can be sprinkled over breakfast cereals and mixed into plain or fruit yogurt.

Health Benefits of Oats: Oats are perhaps the most nutritious of all the grains. Recent research has focused on the ability of oat bran to reduce blood cholesterol (sometimes with dramatic results), while beneficial HDL cholesterol levels increase. For best results, oat bran should be eaten daily at regular intervals.

High in soluble fibre (especially uncooked), oats are an effective laxative and also feature protease inhibitors, a combination that has been found to inhibit certain cancers. Oats also contain vitamin E and some B vitamins, as well as iron, calcium, magnesium, phosphorus and potassium.

RYE

The most popular grain for bread-making in Eastern Europe, Scandinavia and Russia, rye flour produces a dark, dense and dry loaf that keeps well. It is a hardy

Below: Clockwise from top left: rolled oats, oatmeal, whole oats and bran.

Below: Rye grain and flour.

grain, which grows where most others fail – hence its popularity in colder climates. Rye is low in gluten and so rye flour is often mixed with high-gluten

wheat flours to create lighter textured breads, the colour of which may be intensified using molasses. The whole grain can be soaked overnight, then cooked in boiling water until tender, but the flour, with its robust, full flavour and greyish colour, is the most commonly used form. The flour ranges from dark to light, depending on whether the bran and germ have been removed.

Health Benefits of Rye: Rye is a good source of vitamin E and some B vitamins, as well as protein, calcium, iron, phosphorus and potassium. It is also high in fibre, and is used in natural medicine to help to strengthen the digestive system.

CORN

Although we are familiar with yellow corn or maize, blue, red, black and even multi-coloured varieties can also be found. Corn is an essential store-cupboard ingredient in the USA, the Caribbean and Italy, and comes in many forms.

Masa Harina

Maize meal, or masa harina, comes from the cooked whole grain, which is ground into flour and commonly used to make the Mexican flat bread, tortilla.

Cornmeal

The most popular culinary uses for cornmeal are cornbread, a classic, southern American bread, and polenta, which confusingly is both the Italian name for cornmeal as well as a dish made with the grain. Polenta (the cooked dish), or mamaliga as it is known in Romania, is a thick, golden porridge, characteristic of northern Italian cooking. It is often flavoured with butter and cheese, such as Gorgonzola, or chopped herbs. Once cooked, polenta can also be left to cool, then cut into slabs and fried, barbecued or griddled until golden brown. It is delicious with roasted vegetables. Ready made polenta, sold in firm blocks and ready-to-slice, is available from some supermarkets.Polenta grain comes in various grades, ranging from fine to coarse. You can buy polenta that takes 40–45 minutes to cook or an "instant" part-cooked version that can be cooked in less than 5 minutes.

In the Caribbean, cornmeal is used to make puddings and dumplings.

MAKING POLENTA

Polenta makes an excellent alternative to mashed potato or rice. It needs plenty of seasoning and is even better with a knob of butter and cheese, such as Parmesan, Gorgonzola or Taleggio. Serve with stews or casseroles.

1 Pour 1 litre/1¾ pints/4 cups water into a heavy pan and bring to the boil. Remove from the heat.

2 In a steady stream, gradually add 185g/6½oz/1½ cups instant polenta and stir constantly with a balloon whisk to avoid any lumps forming and until incorporated.

3 Return the pan to the heat and cook, stirring continuously with a wooden spoon, until the polenta is thick and creamy and starts to come away from the sides of the pan – this will only take a few minutes if you are using instant polenta.

4 Season to taste, then add a generous knob of butter and mix well. Remove from the heat and stir in the cheese, if using, until melted. The polenta can be served in its soft form or omit the cheese and spoon on to a wet work surface and spread out until 1cm/½ in thick. Leave to cool, then cut into slices.

Right: Clockwise from top left: Blue and yellow cornmeal, cornflour, popcorn, masa harina and polenta.

Cornflour

This fine white powder, also known as cornstarch, is a useful thickening agent for sauces, soups and casseroles. It can also be added to cakes.

Hominy

These are the husked whole grains of corn. They should be cooked in boiling water until softened, then used in stews and soups, or added to cakes and muffins. They are most commonly eaten ground, as grits, in cereals.

Grits

Coarsely ground, dried yellow or white corn is known as grits. Use for porridge and pancakes or add to baked goods.

Popcorn

This is a separate strain of corn that is grown specifically to make the popular snack food. The kernel's hard outer casing explodes when heated. Popcorn can easily be made at home and flavoured sweet or savoury according to taste. The shop-bought types are often high in salt or sugar.

Health Benefits of Corn: In American folk medicine, corn is considered a diuretic and a mild stimulant. Corn is said to prevent cancer of the colon, breast and prostate and to lower the risk of heart disease. It is believed to be the only grain that contains vitamin A as well as some of the B vitamins and iron.

Right:
Quinoa.

Above: Clockwise from top left: pot barley, barley flakes and pearl barley.

BARLEY

Believed to be the oldest cultivated grain, barley is still a fundamental part of the everyday diet in Eastern Europe, the Middle East and Asia.

Pearl barley, the most usual form, is husked, steamed and then polished to give it its characteristic cream-coloured appearance. It has a mild, sweet flavour and chewy texture, and can be added to soups, stews and bakes. It is also used to make traditional barley water.

Pot barley is the whole grain with just the inedible outer husk removed. It takes much longer to cook than pearl barley. Barley flakes, which make a satisfying porridge, barley couscous and barley flour are also available.

Health Benefits of Barley: Pot barley is more nutritious than pearl barley, because it contains extra fibre, calcium, phosphorus, iron, magnesium and B vitamins. Barley was once used to increase potency and boost physical strength. More recently, studies have shown that its fibre content may help to prevent constipation and other digestive problems, as well as heart disease and certain cancers. In addition, the protease inhibitors in barley have been found to suppress cancer of the intestines, and eating barley regularly may also reduce the amount of harmful cholesterol produced by the liver.

QUINOA

Hailed as the supergrain of the future, quinoa (pronounced "keen-wa") is a grain of the past. It was called "the mother grain" by the Incas, who cultivated it for hundreds of years, high in the Andes, solely for their own use.

Nowadays, quinoa is widely available. Although we tend to see the creamy coloured varietys, it's also available in red, black, green and pink. The tiny, bead-shaped grains have a mild, slightly

LEMON BARLEY WATER

INGREDIENTS
225g/8oz/1 cup pearl barley
1.75 litres/3 pints/7½ cups water
grated rind of 1 lemon
50g/2oz/¼ cup golden caster
   (superfine) sugar
juice of 2 lemons

1 Rinse the barley thoroughly in cold water, then place it in a large pan and cover with the water. Bring to the boil, then reduce the heat and simmer gently for 20 minutes, skimming off any scum that rises to the surface from time to time. Remove the pan from the heat.

2 Add the lemon rind and sugar to the pan, stir well and leave to cool. Strain, and add the lemon juice.

3 Taste the lemon barley water and add more sugar, if necessary. Serve chilled with ice and slices of lemon.

bitter taste and firm texture. It is cooked in the same way as rice, but the grains quadruple in size, becoming translucent with an unusual white outer ring. Quinoa is useful for making stuffings, pilaffs, salads, bakes and breakfast cereals.

Health Benefits of Quinoa: Quinoa's supergrain status hails from its rich nutritional value. Unlike most other grains, quinoa is a complete protein because it contains all eight essential amino acids. It is an excellent source of calcium, potassium and zinc as well as iron, magnesium and B vitamins. It is particularly valuable for people with coeliac disease as it is gluten-free.

MILLET

Although millet is usually associated with bird food, it is a highly nutritious grain. It once rivalled barley as the main food of Europe and remains a staple ingredient in many parts of the world, including Africa, China and India. Its mild flavour makes it an ideal accompaniment to spicy stews and

curries, and it can be used as a base for pilaffs or milk puddings. The tiny, firm grains can also be flaked or ground into flour. Millet is gluten-free, so it is a useful food for people with coeliac disease. The flour can be used for baking, but needs to be combined with high-gluten flours to make leavened bread.

Health Benefits of Millet: Millet is an easily digestible grain. It contains more iron than other grains and is a good source of zinc, calcium, manganese and B vitamins. It is believed to be beneficial to those suffering from candidiasis, a fungal infection caused by the yeast *Candida albicans*.

Above: Millet.

Above: Amaranth.

AMARANTH

This plant, which is native to Mexico, is unusual in that it can be eaten as both a vegetable and a grain. Like quinoa, amaranth is considered a supergrain due to its excellent nutritional content. The tiny pale seed or "grain" has a strong and distinctive, peppery flavour. It is best used in stews and soups, or it can be ground into flour to make bread, pastries and biscuits. The flour is gluten-free and has to be mixed with wheat or another flour that contains gluten to make leavened bread. Amaranth leaves are similar to spinach and can be cooked or eaten raw in salads.

Health Benefits of Amaranth: Although its taste may take some getting used to, the nutritional qualities of amaranth more than make up for it. It has more protein than pulses and is rich in amino acids, particularly lysine. Amaranth is also high in iron and calcium.

SORGHUM

This grain is best known for its thick sweet syrup, which is used in cakes and desserts. The grain is similar to millet and is an important, extremely nutritious staple food in Africa and India. It can be used much like rice, and when ground into flour is used to make unleavened bread.

Health Benefits of Sorghum: Sorghum is a useful source of calcium, iron and B vitamins.

Left to right: Plain buckwheat, buckwheat flour and toasted buckwheat.

BUCKWHEAT

In spite of its name, buckwheat is not a type of wheat, but is actually related to the rhubarb family. Available plain or toasted, it has a nutty, earthy flavour. It is a staple food in Eastern Europe as well as Russia, where the triangular grain is milled into a speckled-grey flour and used to make blini. The flour is also used in Japan for soba noodles and in Italy for pasta. Buckwheat pancakes are popular in parts of the USA and France. The whole grain, which is also known as kasha, makes a fine porridge or a creamy pudding.

Health Benefits of Buckwheat: Buckwheat is a complete protein. It has all eight essential amino acids as well as rutin, which aids circulation and helps treat high blood pressure. It is an excellent, sustaining cereal, rich in iron and some of the B complex vitamins. It is also reputed to be good for the lungs, the kidneys and the bladder. Buckwheat is gluten-free, and so is useful for people who suffer from coeliac disease.

TRITICALE

A hybrid of wheat and rye, triticale was created by Swedish researchers in 1875. It has a sweet, nutty taste and chewy texture and can be used in the same way as rice, and is ground into flour. It contains more protein than wheat but has less gluten and may need to be mixed with other flours when baking. Triticale flakes can be used in breakfast cereals and crumbles.

Health Benefits of Triticale: Triticale contains significant amounts of calcium, iron and B vitamins. It is particularly rich in lysine an essential amino acid that must be taken in through the diet.

TEFF

An important grain in Ethiopia, teff is nutritionally similar to millet. This tiny grain is gluten-free and is therefore suitable for those with coeliac disease. Teff is an ancient grain and seeds were even found in a pyramid dating back to 3359BC.

Right: Spelt grain and flour.

Health Benefits of Teff: Teff is a complete protein since it contains all eight essential amino acids and is rich in calcium, iron, phosphorus and thiamine.

Buying and Storing: Buy grains in small quantities from a shop with a high turnover of stock. Grains can be affected by heat and moisture, and easily become rancid. Store in a dry, cool, dark place.

HOW TO COOK GRAINS

All grains can be simply boiled in water to cook them, but, to enhance their flavour, first cook them in a little oil for a few minutes. When they are well coated in oil, add two or three times their volume of water or stock. Bring to the boil, then simmer, covered, until the water is absorbed and the grains are tender. Do not disturb the grains while they are cooking. Other flavourings, such as chopped herbs and whole or ground spices, can be added to the cooking liquid.

Above: Kamut.

FABULOUS FIBRE

Whole grains are one of the few food groups to contain both soluble and insoluble fibre. The former is prevalent in oats and rye, while rice, wheat and corn contain insoluble fibre. Both are fundamental to good health and may help prevent ulcers, constipation, colitis, colon and rectal cancer, heart disease, diverticulitis and irritable bowel syndrome. Soluble fibre slows the absorption of energy from the gut, which means there are no sudden demands on insulin, making it especially important for diabetics as well as those following a low GI diet.

PASTA

Pasta, meaning "dough", is one of the oldest "manufactured" foods, dating back more than 1,000 years, that is still popular today. Top-quality pasta is made from durum wheat and water, or egg, which gives the pasta a richer flavour and golden colour. Gluten free pastas are now widely available, made from various other grains. The variety of shapes is almost endless, from the tiny soup pastas to large shells used for stuffing. Low in fat and high in complex carbohydrates, pasta provides plenty of long-term energy.

Durum Wheat Pasta

When buying pasta look for one that is made with durum wheat. This hard, high-protein wheat produces a fine semolina flour that is called "00" in Italy. The pasta may then include egg or not. Egg pasta, because it is more delicate, is often packed in nests or compressed into waves. Lasagne can be made with either plain or egg pasta. At one time, almost all short pasta shapes were made from plain pasta, but shapes made with egg pasta are now readily available. Pasta made with egg has advantages over plain pasta: it has a higher protein content and many people consider it to have a superior, richer flavour.

Wholewheat Pasta

This substantial pasta is made using wholemeal (whole wheat) flour and it contains more fibre than plain durum wheat pasta. It has a slightly chewy texture and nutty flavour and takes longer to cook. Wholewheat spaghetti (bigoli), a traditional Italian variety that comes from the area around Venice known as the Veneto, can be found in

Right: Spaghetti, linguine and tagliatelle.

good delicatessens, and in supermarkets and helath food stores. There is an increasing range of wholewheat shapes, from tiny soup pastas to rotelle (wheels) and lasagne.

Below: Buckwheat pasta spirals and short cut pasta.

Buckwheat Pasta

Pasta made from buckwheat flour has a nutty taste and is darker in colour than wholewheat pasta. Pizzoccheri from Lombardy is the classic shape. These thin, flat noodles are traditionally sold in nests like tagliatelle (although pizzoccheri are about half the length), but they are also available cut into short strips.

Other buckwheat pasta shapes are available in health food shops and supermarkets. Buckwheat pasta is gluten-free and suitable for people who are intolerant to gluten or wheat. It is also very nutritious, containing all eight amino acids, calcium, zinc and B vitamins.

Corn Pasta

This pasta, made with corn or maize flour, is gluten-free and a good alternative for people who cannot tolerate gluten or wheat. It is made in a wide range of shapes, including fusilli (spirals), spaghetti and conchiglie (shells), as well as more unusual varieties. Plain corn pasta is a sunshine-yellow colour, or may be flavoured with spinach or tomato. It is cooked and used in the same way as wheat pasta and is available from many health food stores.

Coloured and Flavoured Pasta

A variety of ingredients can be added to the pasta dough to give it both flavour and colour. The most common additions are tomato and spinach, but beetroot, saffron, fresh herbs such as basil, and even chocolate are used. Mixed bags of pasta are also available – the traditional

Left: Corn or maize pasta can be bought in a wide variety of shapes from simple elbow macaroni to fusilli and three coloured radiatori.

combination of plain and spinach-flavoured pasta is called *paglia e fieno*, which means straw and hay. But there are many other mixtures, some having as many as seven different flavours and colours of pasta.

Rice Pasta

Like pasta made with corn and buckwheat, rice pasta is gluten-free. It also comes in a range of shapes.

Above: Pasta can be coloured and flavoured in a variety of ways, but plain, spinach and tomato varieties are the most common.

QUICK IDEAS FOR PASTA

• To make a richly flavoured tomato sauce: place some plum or cherry tomatoes in a baking dish and drizzle with a little olive oil. Roast in a hot oven for 15 minutes, then add two peeled garlic cloves and continue roasting for 10 minutes more. Transfer to a food processor and blend with basil leaves. Season and stir into cooked pasta.

• Toss cooked pasta in a little chilli oil, scatter over rocket leaves and pine nuts and serve with finely grated Parmesan cheese.

• Stir a spoonful of black olive tapenade into cooked pasta, then scatter a few lightly toasted walnuts on top.

• Roast a head of garlic, then squeeze out the pulpy cloves and mix with olive oil. Toss with cooked pasta and sprinkle over plenty of fresh, chopped parsley.

• Olives, mushrooms, aubergines (eggplant) and artichokes bottled in olive oil make quick and delicious additions to pasta.

• Combine cooked pasta with small chunks of mozzarella cheese, sliced sun-dried tomatoes, chopped fresh mint and a splash of olive oil.

PASTA SHAPES

Many different shapes of pasta are available and all are suitable for serving with different types of pasta sauces.

Long Pasta

Dried long pasta in the form of spaghetti is probably the best known shape, but there are many other varieties, from fine vermicelli to pappardelle – broad ribbon noodles. Tagliatelle, the most common form of ribbon noodles, is usually sold coiled into nests. Long pasta is best served with a thin sauce, made with olive oil, butter, cream, eggs, grated cheese or chopped fresh herbs. When vegetables are added to the sauce, they should be finely chopped.

Short Pasta

There are hundreds of different short dried pasta shapes, which may be made with plain pasta dough or the egg pasta. Conchiglie (shells) is one of the most useful shapes because it is concave and traps virtually any sauce. Fusilli (spirals) is good with thick tomato-based sauces and farfalle (butterflies) can be served with creamy sauces, but is very versatile and works equally well with tomato- or olive oil-based sauces. Macaroni used to be the most common short shape and, being hollow, it is good for most sauces and baked dishes. However, penne (quills) have become more popular, perhaps because the hollow tubes with diagonally cut ends go well with virtually any sauce. They are particularly good with chunky vegetable sauces or baked with cheese sauce.

Below: Spinach and wholewheat lasagne and plain cannelloni.

Flat Pasta

Lasagne is designed to be baked between layers of sauce, or cooked in boiling water, then layered, or rolled around a filling to make cannelloni. Lasagne is made from plain or egg pasta and both fresh and dried versions are available. The pasta sheets may be flavoured with tomato or spinach, or made with wholewheat flour.

Stuffed Pasta

The most common stuffed pasta shapes are ravioli, tortellini (little pies) and cappelletti (little hats), athough there are other less common shapes available from Italian delicatessens. Plain, spinach and tomato doughs are the most usual, and there is a wide range of vegetarian fillings such as spinach and ricotta, sun-dried tomatoes, mushroom or pumpkin.

Right: Large and small conchiglie pasta.

COOKING PASTA

Pasta should be cooked in a large pan of salted boiling water to allow the strands or shapes to expand, and stirred occasionally to prevent them from sticking together. Do not add oil to the cooking water as it makes the pasta slippery and prevents it from absorbing the sauce. Cooking instructions are given on the packaging but always taste just before the end of the given time to prevent overcooking. Dried pasta should be *al dente*, or firm to the bite, while fresh pasta should be just tender.

Bring a large pan of salted water to the boil. For shapes, tip in the pasta and then cover the pan. Bring quickly back to the boil and remove the lid. Reduce the heat slightly, then stir the pasta and cook according to the instructions on the packet. For long straight pasta, such as spaghetti, coil the pasta into the water as it softens.

Pasta for Soup

These tiny shapes are mostly made from plain durum wheat pasta, though you may find them with egg. There are hundreds of different ones, from tiny risi, which look like grains of rice, to alfabeti (alphabet shapes), which are popular with children. Slightly larger shapes such as farfallini (little bows) and tubetti (little tubes), the more substantial conchigliette (little shells) and farfallini (little butterflies) go well in hearty vegetable soup, such as minestrone.

Right: Fresh tortellini.

Buying and Storing Pasta: The quality of pasta varies tremendously – choose good-quality Italian brands of pasta made from 100 per cent durum wheat, and visit your local Italian delicatessen to buy fresh pasta, rather than buying pre-packed pasta from the supermarket. Dried pasta will keep almost indefinitely, but if you decant the pasta into a storage jar, it is a good idea to use up the remaining pasta before adding any from a new packet. Fresh pasta from a delicatessen is usually sold loose and is best cooked the same day, but can be kept in the refrigerator for a day or two. Fresh pasta from a supermarket is likely to be packed in plastic packs and bags, and these will keep for 3–4 days in the refrigerator. Fresh pasta freezes well and should be cooked from frozen. Packs and bags of supermarket pasta have the advantage of being easy to store in the freezer.

Health Benefits of Pasta: Pasta provides the body with fuel for all kinds of physical activity, from walking to the bus stop to running a marathon. High in complex carbohydrates, pasta is broken down slowly, providing energy over a long period of time. Wholewheat pasta is the most nutritious, containing a richer concentration of vitamins, minerals and fibre. Nevertheless, all pasta is a useful source of protein, as well as being low in fat. Buckwheat is very nutritious; it contains all eight essential amino acids, making it a complete protein. It is also particularly high in fibre.

CHOOSING THE RIGHT SHAPE

• Long pasta shapes, such as spaghetti, linguine, tagliatelle and fettuccine, suit smooth cream, or olive oil-based sauces, or vegetable sauces in which the ingredients are very finely chopped.

• Hollow shapes, such as penne (quills), fusilli (spirals) and macaroni, all work well with more robust sauces, such as cheese, tomato and vegetable.

• Stuffed pasta shapes, such as ravioli and cappelletti, are good with simple sauces made with butter, extra virgin olive oil or tomatoes.

• Delicate small shapes, risi (rice), orzi (barley) and quadrucci (squares), suit lighter broths.

Above: Tiny soup pasta is available in hundreds of different shapes.

NOODLES

THE FAST FOOD OF THE EAST, NOODLES CAN BE MADE FROM WHEAT FLOUR, RICE, BUCKWHEAT FLOUR OR MUNG BEAN FLOUR. BOTH FRESH AND DRIED NOODLES ARE READILY AVAILABLE IN HEALTH FOOD STORES AND ASIAN SHOPS AS WELL AS SUPERMARKETS. LIKE PASTA, NOODLES ARE LOW IN FAT AND HIGH IN COMPLEX CARBOHYDRATES, SO PROVIDE LONG-TERM ENERGY.

Wheat Noodles

There are two main types of noodle: plain and egg. Plain noodles are made from strong flour and water, they can be flat or round and come in various thicknesses.

Udon Noodles

These thick Japanese noodles can be round or flat and are available fresh, pre-cooked or dried. Wholewheat udon noodles have a more robust flavour.

Somen Noodles

Usually sold in bundles, held together by a paper band, these thin, white noodles are available from oriental stores.

Egg Noodles

These noodles are sold both fresh and dried. The Chinese type come in various thicknesses. Very fine egg noodles, which resemble vermicelli, are usually sold in coils. Wholewheat egg noodles are widely available from larger supermarkets.

Ramen Noodles

These Japanese egg noodles are also sold in coils and are often cooked and served in a broth.

Left: Rice noodles.

Rice Noodles

These fine, delicate noodles are made from rice and are opaque-white in colour. Like wheat noodles, they come in various widths, from the very thin strands known as rice vermicelli, which are popular in Thailand and southern China, to the thicker rice sticks, which are used more in Vietnam and Malaysia. A huge range of rice noodles is available dried from oriental grocers. Fresh noodles are occasionally found in the chiller cabinets. Since all rice noodles are pre-cooked, they need only to be soaked in hot water for a few minutes to soften them. Drain well and rinse under cold running water before use in stir-fries and salads.

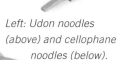

Left: Udon noodles (above) and cellophane noodles (below).

Cellophane Vermicelli and Noodles

Made from mung bean starch, these translucent noodles, also known as bean thread vermicelli and glass noodles, come in a variety of thicknesses and are only available dried. Although very fine, the strands are firm and fairly tough. Cellophane noodles don't need to be boiled, and are simply soaked in boiling water for 10–15 minutes. They have a firm texture, which they retain when cooked, never becoming soggy. Cellophane noodles are almost tasteless unless combined with other strongly flavoured foods and seasonings, so they are never eaten on their own, but used as an ingredient. They are good in vegetarian dishes, and as an ingredient in spring rolls.

Soba Noodles

The best-known type of buckwheat noodle is the soba noodle. They are much darker in colour than wheat noodles – almost brownish grey. In apan, soba noodles are traditionally served in soups or stir-fries with a variety of seasonings and sauces.

Above: Dried and fresh egg noodles.

QUICK IDEAS FOR NOODLES

• To make a broth, dissolve mugi miso in hot water, add cooked soba noodles; sprinkle with chilli flakes and sliced spring onions (scallions).

• Cook ramen noodles in vegetable stock, then add a splash of dark soy sauce, shredded spinach and grated ginger. Sprinkle with sesame seeds and fresh coriander (cilantro).

• Stir-fry sliced shiitake and oyster mushrooms in garlic and ginger, then toss with rice or egg noodles (above). Sprinkle with fresh chives and a little roasted sesame oil.
• In a food processor, blend together some lemon grass, chilli, garlic, ginger, kaffir lime leaves and fresh coriander (cilantro). Fry the paste in sunflower oil and combine with cooked ribbon noodles. Sprinkle on top fresh basil and chopped spring onions (scallions) before serving.

Buying and Storing Noodles: Packets of fresh noodles are found in the chiller cabinets of Asian shops. They usually carry a use-by date and must be stored in the refrigerator. Dried noodles will keep for many months if stored in an airtight container in a cool, dry place.

Health Benefits of Noodles: Wholewheat noodles are high in complex carbohydrates, which are broken down slowly, providing energy over a long period of time. They are also the most nutritious, containing a richer concentration of vitamins, minerals and fibre. Nevertheless, some noodles are a useful source of protein, as well as being low in fat. Buckwheat noodles are made from buckwheat flour, which contains all eight essential amino acids, making it a complete protein. It is also particularly high in fibre. Cellophane noodles are made from mung bean starch, which is reputed to be one of the most effective detoxifiers.

Below: Wholewheat egg noodles.

COOKING WHEAT NOODLES

Wheat noodles are very easy to cook. Both dried and fresh noodles are cooked in a large pan of boiling water; how long depends on the type of noodle and the thickness of the strips. Dried noodles need about 3 minutes cooking time, while fresh ones will often be ready in less than a minute. Fresh noodles may need to be rinsed quickly in cold water to prevent them from overcooking.

BREAKFAST

Often called the most important meal of the day, breakfast replenishes energy and nutrients depleted overnight. Grains, especially the wholegrain variety, are complex carbohydrates and provide plenty of long-term energy, and adding fruit, milk, eggs, or even meat or fish, makes up a nutrient-filled start to the day.

WHEAT BRAN SMOOTHIE

EASY TO PREPARE AND EVEN EASIER TO DRINK, THIS ENERGY-PACKED SMOOTHIE MAKES A GREAT START TO THE DAY. WHEAT BRAN AND BANANAS PROVIDE THE PERFECT FUEL IN THE FORM OF SLOW-RELEASE CARBOHYDRATE THAT WILL KEEP YOU GOING ALL MORNING, WHILE FRESH AND ZESTY ORANGE JUICE AND SWEET, SCENTED MANGO WILL PROVIDE VALUABLE VITAMINS.

MAKES TWO GLASSES

INGREDIENTS
½ mango
1 banana
1 large orange
30ml/2 tbsp wheat bran
15ml/1 tbsp sesame seeds
10–15ml/2–3tsp honey

COOK'S TIP
Mango juice is naturally very sweet so you may wish to add less honey or leave it out altogether. Taste the drink to decide how much you need.

1 Using a small, sharp knife, skin the mango, then slice the flesh off the stone (pit). Peel the banana and break it into short lengths, then place it in a blender or food processor with the mango.

2 Squeeze the juice from the orange and add to the blender or food processor along with the bran, sesame seeds and honey. Whizz until the mixture is smooth and creamy, then pour into glasses and serve.

Energy 172kcal/726kJ; Protein 4.9g; Carbohydrate 27.6g, of which sugars 23.1g; Fat 5.5g, of which saturates 0.9g; Cholesterol 0mg; Calcium 102mg; Fibre 8.5g; Sodium 11mg.

MUESLI SMOOTHIE

THIS STORE-CUPBOARD SMOOTHIE IS PACKED WITH HEALTHY INGREDIENTS AND IS AN INNOVATIVE WAY OF USING MUESLI. ANY EXTRA DRINK CAN BE STORED OVERNIGHT IN THE REFRIGERATOR, ALTHOUGH YOU'LL PROBABLY NEED TO ADD MORE MILK IN THE MORNING AS IT WILL UNDOUBTEDLY THICKEN ON STANDING. IT'S HARD TO BELIEVE THAT SOMETHING SO HEALTHY CAN BE THIS DELICIOUS.

MAKES TWO GLASSES

INGREDIENTS
1 piece preserved stem ginger, plus 30ml/2 tbsp syrup from the ginger jar
50g/2oz/¼ cup ready-to-eat dried apricots, halved or quartered
40g/1½oz/scant ½ cup natural muesli (granola)
about 200ml/7fl oz/scant 1 cup semi-skimmed (low-fat) milk

COOK'S TIP
Apricot and ginger are perfect partners in this divine drink. It makes an incredibly healthy, tasty breakfast, but is so delicious and indulgent that you could even serve it as a dessert after a summer meal.

1 Chop the preserved ginger and put it in a blender or food processor with the syrup, apricots, muesli and milk.

2 Process until smooth, adding more milk if necessary. Serve in wide glasses.

COOK'S TIP
Choose unsulphured dried apricots for the healthiest choice of dried fruit.

Energy 204kcal/865kJ; Protein 6.6g; Carbohydrate 39.1g, of which sugars 28.8g; Fat 3.4g, of which saturates 1.4g; Cholesterol 6mg; Calcium 150mg; Fibre 3.1g; Sodium 97mg.

RASPBERRY AND OATMEAL SMOOTHIE

Just a spoonful or so of high-fibre oatmeal gives substance to this tangy, invigorating drink. If you can, prepare it ahead of time because soaking the raw oats helps to break down the starch into natural sugars, making the drink easier to digest. The smoothie will thicken up in the refrigerator so you might need to stir in a little extra milk or fruit juice just before serving. Using frozen raspberries is economical and convenient.

MAKES ONE LARGE GLASS

INGREDIENTS
25ml/1½ tbsp medium oatmeal
150g/5oz/scant 1 cup raspberries
5–10ml/1–2 tsp clear honey
45ml/3 tbsp natural (plain) yogurt

1 Spoon the oatmeal into a heatproof bowl. Pour in 120ml/4fl oz/½ cup boiling water and leave to stand for about 10 minutes.

2 Put the soaked oats in a blender or food processor and add all but two or three of the raspberries, the honey and about 30ml/2 tbsp of the yogurt. Process until smooth, scraping down the side of the bowl if necessary.

3 Pour the raspberry and oatmeal smoothie into a large glass, swirl in the remaining yogurt and top with the reserved raspberries.

COOK'S TIPS
• If you don't like raspberry pips (seeds) in your smoothies, press the fruit through a sieve with the back of a wooden spoon to make a smooth purée, then process with the oatmeal and yogurt as before.
• Alternatively, try using redcurrants or strawberries instead of the raspberries.
• Although a steaming bowl of porridge can't be beaten as a winter warmer, this smooth, oaty drink makes a great, light alternative in warmer months. It is a good way to make sure you get your fill of wholesome oats for breakfast.

Energy 192kcal/817kJ; Protein 7.5g; Carbohydrate 36.1g, of which sugars 17.9g; Fat 3.1g, of which saturates 0.4g; Cholesterol 1mg; Calcium 137mg; Fibre 5.5g; Sodium 51mg.

WHEATGRASS TONIC

THE NUTRITIONAL BENEFITS OF WHEATGRASS ARE ENORMOUS. IT IS GROWN FROM WHOLEWHEAT GRAIN AND IS A CONCENTRATED SOURCE OF CHLOROPHYLL, WHICH IS A POWERFUL DETOXIFIER, AND ALSO PROVIDES ENZYMES, VITAMINS AND MINERALS. IT HAS A DISTINCTIVE FLAVOUR SO IN THIS JUICE IT IS BLENDED WITH MILD WHITE CABBAGE, BUT IT IS JUST AS TASTY COMBINED WITH OTHER VEGETABLES INSTEAD. ONCE MADE, THIS JUICE SHOULD BE DRUNK WITHIN 15 MINUTES.

MAKES ONE SMALL GLASS

INGREDIENTS
  50g/2oz white cabbage
  90g/3½oz wheatgrass

1 Using a small, sharp knife, roughly shred the cabbage.

2 Push through a juicer with the wheatgrass. Pour the juice into a small glass and serve immediately.

Energy 36kcal/149kJ; Protein 3.2g; Carbohydrate 3.9g, of which sugars 3.8g; Fat 0.8g, of which saturates 0.1g; Cholesterol 0mg; Calcium 178mg; Fibre 2.9g; Sodium 130mg.

TRADITIONAL PORRIDGE

PORRIDGE REMAINS A FAVOURITE WAY TO START THE DAY, ESPECIALLY DURING WINTER. OATMEAL IS RICH IN FIBRE, AND OATS IN GENERAL HAVE BEEN FOUND TO REDUCE HARMFUL BLOOD CHOLESTEROL LEVELS. A SPOONFUL OF BROWN SUGAR OR HONEY AND CREAM ARE ADDITIONAL TREATS.

SERVES FOUR

INGREDIENTS
1 litre/1¾ pints/4 cups water
115g/4oz/1 cup pinhead oatmeal
good pinch of salt

VARIATION
Rolled oats can be used, in the proportion of 115g/4oz/1 cup rolled oats to 750ml/1¼ pints/3 cups water, plus a sprinkling of salt. This cooks more quickly than pinhead oatmeal. Simmer, stirring to prevent the porridge from sticking, for about 5 minutes. Either type of oatmeal can be left to cook overnight in the slow oven of a range.

1 Put the water, pinhead oatmeal and salt into a heavy pan and bring to the boil over a medium heat, stirring with a wooden spatula. When the porridge is smooth and beginning to thicken, reduce the heat to a simmer.

2 Cook gently for about 25 minutes, stirring occasionally, until the oatmeal is cooked and the consistency smooth.

3 Serve hot with cold milk and extra salt, if required.

Energy 115kcal/488kJ; Protein 3.6g; Carbohydrate 20.9g, of which sugars 0g; Fat 2.5g, of which saturates 0g; Cholesterol 0mg; Calcium 16mg; Fibre 2g; Sodium 304mg.

OATMEAL PANCAKES <u>WITH</u> BACON

THESE OATY PANCAKES HAVE A SPECIAL AFFINITY WITH GOOD BACON, MAKING AN INTERESTING BASE FOR AN ALTERNATIVE TO THE BIG TRADITIONAL FRY-UP. SERVE WITH SAUSAGES, FRIED OR POACHED EGGS AND COOKED TOMATOES FOR A HEARTY BREAKFAST.

MAKES EIGHT PANCAKES

INGREDIENTS
    115g/4oz/1 cups wholemeal (whole-
        wheat) flour
    25g/1oz/¼ cup fine pinhead oatmeal
    pinch of salt
    2 eggs
    about 300ml/½ pint/1¼ cups
        buttermilk
    butter or oil, for greasing
    8 bacon rashers (strips)

COOK'S TIP
When whole oats are chopped into pieces they are called pinhead or coarse oatmeal. They take longer to cook than rolled oats and have a chewier texture.

1 Mix the flour, oatmeal and salt in a bowl or food processor, beat in the eggs and add enough buttermilk to make a creamy batter of the same consistency as ordinary pancakes.

2 Thoroughly heat a griddle or cast-iron frying pan over a medium-hot heat. When very hot, grease lightly with butter or oil.

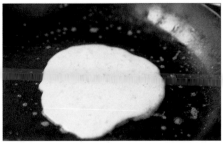

3 Pour in the batter, about a ladleful at a time. Tilt the pan around to spread the batter evenly and cook for about 2 minutes on the first side, or until set and the underside is browned. Turn over and cook for 1 minute until browned. Fry the bacon and roll in the cooked pancakes.

Energy 202kcal/845kJ; Protein 11.9g; Carbohydrate 17.8g, of which sugars 2g; Fat 11.8g, of which saturates 4.8g; Cholesterol 87mg; Calcium 59mg; Fibre 1.5g; Sodium 654mg.

LUXURY MUESLI

COMMERCIALLY MADE MUESLI REALLY CAN'T COMPETE WITH THIS HOME-MADE VERSION. THIS COMBINATION OF SEEDS, GRAINS, NUTS AND DRIED FRUITS WORKS PARTICULARLY WELL, BUT YOU CAN ALTER THE BALANCE OF INGREDIENTS, OR SUBSTITUTE OTHERS, IF YOU LIKE.

SERVES FOUR

INGREDIENTS
   50g/2oz/½ cup sunflower seeds
   25g/1oz/¼ cup pumpkin seeds
   115g/4oz/1 cup rolled oats
   115g/4oz/heaped 1 cup wheat flakes
   115g/4oz/heaped 1 cup barley flakes
   115g/4oz/1 cup raisins
   115g/4oz/1 cup chopped hazelnuts,
      roasted
   115g/4oz/½ cup unsulphured dried
      apricots, chopped
   50g/2oz/2 cups dried apple
      slices, halved
   25g/1oz/⅓ cup desiccated (dry,
      unsweetened shredded) coconut

1 Put the sunflower and pumpkin seeds in a dry frying pan and cook over a medium heat for 3 minutes until golden, tossing the seeds regularly to prevent them from burning.

2 Mix the toasted seeds with the remaining ingredients and leave to cool. Store in an airtight container.

Energy 787kcal/3310kJ; Protein 20g; Carbohydrate 104.4g, of which sugars 38.7g; Fat 35.1g, of which saturates 5.7g; Cholesterol 0mg; Calcium 137mg; Fibre 14g; Sodium 60mg.

GRANOLA

HONEY-COATED NUTS, SEEDS AND OATS, COMBINED WITH SWEET DRIED FRUITS, MAKE AN EXCELLENT AND NUTRITIOUS START TO THE DAY — WITHOUT THE ADDITIVES OFTEN FOUND IN PRE-PACKED CEREALS. SERVE THE GRANOLA WITH SEMI-SKIMMED MILK OR NATURAL LIVE YOGURT AND FRESH FRUIT.

SERVES FOUR

INGREDIENTS
   115g/4oz/1 cup rolled oats
   115g/4oz/1 cup jumbo oats
   50g/2oz/½ cup sunflower seeds
   25g/1oz/2 tbsp sesame seeds
   50g/2oz/½ cup hazelnuts, roasted
   25g/1oz/¼ cup almonds, roughly
      chopped
   50ml/2fl oz/¼ cup sunflower oil
   50ml/2fl oz/¼ cup clear honey
   50g/2oz/½ cup raisins
   50g/2oz/½ cup dried sweetened
      cranberries

1 Preheat the oven to 140°C/275°F/ Gas 1. Mix together the oats, seeds and nuts in a bowl.

COOK'S TIPS
• Try varying the grains, nuts, seeds and dried fruit in this recipe, depending on personal taste.
• For a delicious dessert, serve the granola layered in a glass with fresh fruit and fromage frais or yogurt.

2 Heat the oil and honey in a large pan until melted, then remove the pan from the heat. Add the oat mixture and stir well. Spread out on one or two baking sheets.

3 Bake for about 40–50 minutes until crisp, stirring occasionally to prevent the mixture from sticking. Remove from the oven and mix in the raisins and cranberries. Leave to cool, then store in an airtight container.

Energy 614kcal/2573kJ; Protein 14.4g; Carbohydrate 72.3g, of which sugars 27.9g; Fat 31.6g, of which saturates 2.6g; Cholesterol 0mg; Calcium 132mg; Fibre 6.9g; Sodium 39mg.

OAT AND RAISIN DROP SCONES

SERVE THESE EASY-TO-MAKE ORGANIC SCONES FOR A SPECIAL BREAKFAST OR BRUNCH WITH REAL MAPLE SYRUP OR CLEAR HONEY. THEY SHOULD BE EATEN THE DAY THEY ARE MADE.

MAKES ABOUT SIXTEEN

INGREDIENTS

75g/3oz/⅔ cup self-raising
   (self-rising) flour
2.5ml/½ tsp baking powder
50g/2oz/scant ½ cup raisins
25g/1oz/¼ cup fine oatmeal
25g/1oz/2 tbsp unrefined caster
   (superfine) sugar or rapadura
grated rind of 1 orange
2 egg yolks
10g/¼oz/½ tbsp unsalted (sweet)
   butter or non-hydrogenated
   margarine, melted
200ml/7fl oz/scant 1 cup single
   (light) cream or soya cream
200ml/7fl oz/scant 1 cup water
sunflower oil, for greasing
icing (confectioner's) sugar,
   for dusting

1 Sift the self-raising flour and baking powder together into a large mixing bowl.

2 Add the raisins, oatmeal, sugar and orange rind. Gradually beat in the egg yolks, butter, cream and water to make a creamy batter.

COOK'S TIP
Wrap the cooked scones in a clean dishtowel to keep them soft.

3 Lightly grease and heat a large heavy frying pan or griddle and drop about 30ml/2 tbsp of batter at a time on to the pan or griddle to make six or seven small pancakes.

4 Cook over a moderate heat until bubbles show on the scones' surface, then turn them over and cook for a further 2 minutes until golden.

5 Transfer to a plate and dust with icing sugar. Keep warm while cooking the remaining mixture. Serve warm.

Energy 73kcal/306kJ; Protein 1.5g; Carbohydrate 8.8g, of which sugars 4.1g; Fat 3.8g, of which saturates 2.1g; Cholesterol 33mg; Calcium 34mg; Fibre 0.3g; Sodium 28mg.

WHOLEMEAL BREAKFAST SCONES

THESE UNUSUALLY LIGHT SCONES, MADE FROM A COMBINATION OF WHITE AND WHOLEMEAL FLOUR, ARE VIRTUALLY FAT-FREE SO THEY MUST BE EATEN VERY FRESH. SERVE WITH HIGH-QUALITY BUTTER.

MAKES ABOUT SIXTEEN

INGREDIENTS
  225g/8oz/2 cups plain (all-purpose)
  flour
  2.5ml/½ tsp bicarbonate of soda
  (baking soda)
  2.5ml/½ tsp salt
  225g/8oz/2 cups wholemeal (wholewheat) flour
  about 350ml/12fl oz/1½ cups
  buttermilk or sour cream and
  milk mixed
  topping (optional): egg wash (1 egg
  yolk mixed with 15ml/1 tbsp water),
  or a little grated cheese

VARIATION
For a traditional scone mixture that
keeps longer, rub 50g/2oz/¼ cup butter
into the dry ingredients. Increase the
proportion of the soda to 5ml/1 tsp, as
the scones will not be as light.

1 Preheat the oven to 220°C/425°F/
Gas 7. Oil and flour a baking tray.
Sift the plain flour, bicarbonate of soda
and salt in a bowl, add the wholemeal
flour and mix. Make a well in the
centre, pour in almost all the liquid and
mix, adding the remaining liquid as
needed to make a soft, moist dough.
Do not overmix.

2 Lightly dust a work surface with flour,
turn out the dough and dust the top
with flour; press out evenly to a
thickness of 4cm/1½in. Cut out about
16 scones with a 5cm/2in fluted pastry
(cookie) cutter. Place on the baking tray
and then brush the tops with egg wash,
or sprinkle with a little grated cheese,
if using.

3 Bake for about 12 minutes until well
risen and golden brown.

Energy 117Kcal/493kJ; Protein 3.8g; Carbohydrate 20.9g, of which sugars 1.5g; Fat 2.6g, of which saturates 1.4g; Cholesterol 6mg; Calcium 49mg; Fibre 1.7g; Sodium 72mg.

WHOLEWHEAT FRUITY BREAKFAST BARS

INSTEAD OF BUYING FRUIT AND CEREAL BARS FROM THE SUPERMARKET, TRY MAKING THIS QUICK AND EASY VERSION — THEY ARE MUCH TASTIER AND SINCE THEY ARE MADE WITH WHOLEMEAL FLOUR, THEY ARE FULL OF FIBRE AND OTHER BENEFICIAL NUTRIENTS. STORE IN AN AIRTIGHT CONTAINER.

MAKES TWELVE

INGREDIENTS

  270g/10oz jar apple sauce
  115g/4oz/½ cup ready-to-eat dried
    apricots, chopped
  115g/4oz/¾ cup raisins
  50g/2oz/¼ cup demerara (raw) sugar
  50g/2oz/⅓ cup sunflower seeds
  25g/1oz/2 tbsp sesame seeds
  25g/1oz/¼ cup pumpkin seeds
  75g/3oz/scant 1 cup rolled oats
  75g/3oz/⅔ cup self-raising
    (self-rising) wholemeal (whole-
    wheat) flour
  50g/2oz/⅔ cup desiccated (dry
    unsweetened shredded) coconut
  2 eggs, beaten

COOK'S TIP
Allow the baking parchment to hang over the edges of the tin; this makes the baked bars easier to remove.

1 Preheat the oven to 200°C/400°F/ Gas 6. Grease a 20cm/8in square shallow baking tin (pan) and line with baking parchment.

2 Put the apple sauce in a large bowl with the apricots, raisins, sugar and the sunflower, sesame and pumpkin seeds. Stir together with a wooden spoon until thoroughly mixed.

3 Add the oats, flour, coconut and eggs to the fruit mixture and gently stir together until evenly combined.

4 Turn the mixture into the tin and spread to the edges in an even layer. Bake for about 25 minutes or until golden and just firm to the touch.

5 Leave to cool in the tin, then lift out on to a board and cut into bars.

Energy 207kcal/871kJ; Protein 4.9g; Carbohydrate 29.6g, of which sugars 19.3g; Fat 8.5g, of which saturates 3g; Cholesterol 32mg; Calcium 67mg; Fibre 2.8g; Sodium 46mg.

BASMATI RICE KEDGEREE

THIS CLASSIC DISH ORIGINATED IN INDIA. IT IS BEST MADE WITH BASMATI RICE, WHICH GOES WELL WITH THE MILD CURRY FLAVOUR, BUT LONG GRAIN RICE WILL DO. FOR A COLOURFUL GARNISH, ADD SOME FINELY SLICED RED ONION AND RED ONION MARMALADE — IDEAL FOR A LUXURIOUS BRUNCH.

SERVES FOUR

INGREDIENTS
  450g/1lb undyed smoked
    haddock fillet
  750ml/1¼ pints/3 cups milk
  2 bay leaves
  ½ lemon, sliced
  50g/2oz/¼ cup butter
  1 onion, chopped
  2.5ml/½ tsp ground turmeric
  5ml/1 tsp mild Madras curry powder
  2 green cardamom pods, split
  350g/12oz/1¾ cups basmati or long
    grain rice, washed and drained
  4 hard-boiled eggs (not *too* hard),
    roughly chopped
  150ml/¼ pint/⅔ cup single (light)
    cream or Greek (US strained plain)
    yogurt
  30ml/2 tbsp chopped fresh parsley
  salt and ground black pepper

1 Put the haddock in a shallow pan and add the milk, bay leaves and lemon slices. Poach gently for 8–10 minutes, until the haddock flakes easily when tested with the tip of a sharp knife. Strain the milk into a jug, discarding the bay leaves and lemon slices. Remove the skin from the flesh of the haddock, and flake the flesh into large pieces. Keep hot until required.

2 Melt the butter in the pan, add the onion and cook over a low heat for about 3 minutes, until softened. Stir in the turmeric, the curry powder and cardamom pods and fry for 1 minute.

3 Add the rice, stirring to coat it well with the butter. Pour in the reserved milk, stir and bring to the boil. Lower the heat and simmer the rice for 10–12 minutes, until all the milk has been absorbed and the rice is tender. Season to taste.

4 Gently stir in the fish and hard-boiled eggs, with the cream or yogurt, if using. Sprinkle with the parsley and serve.

VARIATION
Use smoked or poached fresh salmon for a delicious change from haddock.

Energy 582kcal/2431kJ; Protein 34.7g; Carbohydrate 71.4g, of which sugars 1.2g; Fat 17.1g, of which saturates 8.2g; Cholesterol 257mg; Calcium 101mg; Fibre 0.8g; Sodium 1005mg.

KITCHIRI

THIS SPICY LENTIL AND RICE DISH IS A VEGETARION VARIATION OF THE ORIGINAL INDIAN DISH KEDGEREE. SERVE IT AS IT IS, OR TOPPED WITH QUARTERED HARD-BOILED EGGS IF YOU'D LIKE TO ADD MORE PROTEIN. IT IS ALSO DELICIOUS SERVED ON GRILLED, LARGE FIELD MUSHROOMS.

SERVES FOUR

INGREDIENTS
  50g/2oz/¼ cup dried red lentils,
    rinsed
  1 bay leaf
  225g/8oz/1 cup basmati rice, rinsed
  4 cloves
  50g/2oz/4 tbsp butter
  5ml/1 tsp curry powder
  2.5ml/½ tsp mild chilli powder
  30ml/2 tbsp chopped flat leaf parsley
  salt and ground black pepper
  4 hard-boiled eggs, quartered, to
    serve (optional)

1 Put the lentils in a pan, add the bay leaf and cover with cold water. Bring to the boil, skim off any foam, then reduce the heat. Cover and simmer for 25–30 minutes, until tender. Drain, then discard the bay leaf.

2 Meanwhile, place the rice in a pan and cover with 475ml/16fl oz/2 cups boiling water. Add the cloves and a generous pinch of salt. Cook, covered, for 10–15 minutes, until all the water is absorbed and the rice is tender. Discard the cloves.

3 Melt the butter in a large frying pan over a gentle heat, then add the curry and chilli powders and cook for 1 minute.

4 Stir in the lentils and rice and mix well until they are coated in the spiced butter. Season and cook for 1–2 minutes until heated through. Stir in the parsley and serve with the hard-boiled eggs, if using.

Energy 339kcal/1414kJ; Protein 7.6g; Carbohydrate 52.4g, of which sugars 0.7g; Fat 10.9g, of which saturates 6.5g; Cholesterol 27mg; Calcium 44mg; Fibre 1.3g; Sodium 85mg.

HERRINGS IN OATMEAL WITH BACON

THIS DELICIOUS DISH IS CHEAP AND NUTRITIOUS. FOR EASE OF EATING, BONE THE HERRINGS BEFORE COATING THEM IN THE OATMEAL. IF YOU DON'T LIKE HERRINGS, USE TROUT OR MACKEREL INSTEAD. FOR EXTRA COLOUR AND FLAVOUR, SERVE WITH GRILLED TOMATOES.

SERVES FOUR

INGREDIENTS

115–150g/4–5oz/1–1¼ cups
  medium oatmeal
10ml/2 tsp mustard powder
4 herrings, about 225g/8oz each,
  cleaned, boned, heads and
  tails removed
30ml/2 tbsp sunflower oil
8 rindless streaky (fatty) bacon
  rashers (strips)
salt and ground black pepper
lemon wedges, to serve

COOK'S TIPS
• Use tongs to turn the herrings so as not to dislodge the oatmeal.
• Cook the herrings two at a time.
• Don't overcrowd the frying pan.

1 In a shallow dish, mix together the oatmeal and mustard powder with salt and pepper. Press the herrings into the mixture one at a time to coat them thickly on both sides. Shake off the excess oatmeal mixture and set the herrings aside.

2 Heat the oil in a large frying pan and fry the bacon until crisp. Drain on kitchen paper and keep hot.

3 Put the herrings into the pan and fry them for 3–4 minutes on each side, until crisp and golden brown. Serve the herrings with the streaky bacon rashers and lemon wedges.

Energy 700kcal/2917kJ; Protein 51.9g; Carbohydrate 20.9g, of which sugars 0g; Fat 46g, of which saturates 11.2g; Cholesterol 139mg; Calcium 153mg; Fibre 2g; Sodium 1050mg.

SOUPS AND
APPETIZERS

Grains lend themselves very well to soups,
whether it be a hearty farmhouse Beef and
Barley Soup or a lighter, fragrant Spicy
Couscous and Shellfish Broth. Many of the
appetizers include flavours from around the
world, from Italian Polenta Fritters to
Japanese Simple Rolled Sushi.

LENTIL AND PASTA SOUP

THE PASTA IN THIS RUSTIC VEGETARIAN SOUP MAKES IT A HEARTY AND WARMING MEAL, WITH A GOOD BALANCE OF CARBOHYDRATES AND PROTEIN. ADD BABY BROAD BEANS IF THEY ARE IN SEASON.

SERVES FOUR TO SIX

INGREDIENTS

175g/6oz/³/₄ cup brown lentils
3 garlic cloves, unpeeled
1 litre/1³/₄ pints/4 cups water
45ml/3 tbsp olive oil
25g/1oz/2 tbsp butter
1 onion, finely chopped
2 celery sticks, finely chopped
30ml/2 tbsp sun-dried tomato
  purée (paste)
1.75 litres/3 pints/7¹/₂ cups
  vegetable stock
a few fresh marjoram leaves
a few fresh basil leaves
leaves from 1 fresh thyme sprig
50g/2oz/¹/₂ cup dried small pasta
  shapes, such as macaroni or tubetti
salt and ground black pepper
tiny fresh herb leaves, to garnish

1 Put the lentils in a large pan. Smash one of the garlic cloves using the blade of a large knife (there's no need to peel it first), then add it to the lentils. Pour in the water and bring to the boil. Simmer for about 20 minutes, or until the lentils are tender. Drain the lentils in a sieve, remove the garlic and set it aside. Rinse the lentils under the cold tap and leave to drain.

2 Heat 30ml/2 tbsp of the oil with half the butter in the pan. Add the onion and celery and cook gently for 5 minutes.

3 Crush the remaining garlic, then peel and mash the reserved garlic. Add to the pan with the remaining oil, the tomato purée and the lentils. Stir, then add the stock, herbs and salt and pepper. Bring to the boil, stirring. Simmer for 30 minutes, stirring occasionally.

4 Add the pasta and bring the soup back to the boil, stirring. Reduce the heat and simmer until the pasta is just tender. Add the remaining butter to the pan and stir until melted. Taste the soup for seasoning, then serve hot in warmed bowls, sprinkled with the fresh herb leaves.

Energy 179kcal/753kJ; Protein 8.4g; Carbohydrate 24.2g, of which sugars 2.3g; Fat 6.1g, of which saturates 0.9g; Cholesterol 0mg; Calcium 25mg; Fibre 2.1g; Sodium 29mg.

BRAISED BEAN AND WHEAT SOUP

THIS DISH IS WONDERFULLY EASY TO MAKE, BUT IT IS VITAL THAT YOU SOAK THE PULSES AND WHEAT THE DAY BEFORE YOU SERVE IT. OFFER EXTRA VIRGIN OLIVE OIL WITH IT AT THE TABLE.

SERVES FOUR

INGREDIENTS

- 200g/7oz/1¼ cups mixed beans and lentils
- 25g/1oz/2 tbsp whole wheat grains
- 150ml/¼ pint/⅔ cup extra virgin olive oil
- 1 large onion, finely chopped
- 2 garlic cloves, crushed
- 5–6 fresh sage leaves, chopped
- juice of 1 lemon
- 3 spring onions (scallions), thinly sliced
- 60–75ml/4–5 tbsp chopped fresh dill
- salt and ground black pepper

1 Put the pulses and wheat in a large bowl and cover with cold water. Leave to soak overnight.

2 Next day, drain the pulse mixture, rinse it under cold water and drain again. Put the mixture in a large pan. Cover with plenty of cold water and cook for about 1½ hours, by which time all the ingredients will be quite soft.

3 Strain the bean mixture, reserving 475ml/16fl oz/2 cups of the cooking liquid. Return the bean mixture to the clean pan.

4 Heat the oil in a frying pan and fry the onion until light golden. Add the garlic and sage. As soon as the garlic becomes aromatic, add the mixture to the beans. Stir in the reserved liquid, add plenty of seasoning and simmer for about 15 minutes, or until the pulses are piping hot. Stir in the lemon juice, then spoon into serving bowls, top with a sprinkling of spring onions and dill and serve.

Energy 442kcal/1844kJ; Protein 14.1g; Carbohydrate 39.2g, of which sugars 5.9g; Fat 26.5g, of which saturates 3.7g; Cholesterol 0mg; Calcium 76mg; Fibre 4.7g; Sodium 27mg.

TOMATO SOUP WITH ISRAELI COUSCOUS

ISRAELI COUSCOUS IS A TOASTED ROUND PASTA, WHICH IS MUCH LARGER THAN REGULAR COUSCOUS. IT MAKES A WONDERFUL ADDITION TO THIS WARM AND COMFORTING SOUP.

SERVES FOUR TO SIX

INGREDIENTS
  30ml/2 tbsp olive oil
  1 onion, chopped
  1–2 carrots, diced
  400g/14oz can chopped tomatoes
  6 garlic cloves, roughly chopped
  1.5 litres/2½ pints/6¼ cups
    vegetable or chicken stock
  200–250g/7–9oz/1–1½ cups
    Israeli couscous
  2–3 mint sprigs, chopped, or several
    pinches of dried mint
  1.5ml/¼ tsp ground cumin
  ¼ bunch fresh coriander (cilantro),
    or about 5 sprigs, chopped
  cayenne pepper, to taste
  salt and ground black pepper

1 Heat the oil in a large pan, add the onion and carrots and cook gently for about 10 minutes until softened. Add the tomatoes, half the garlic, the stock, couscous, mint, ground cumin, coriander, and cayenne pepper, salt and pepper to taste.

2 Bring the soup to the boil, add the remaining chopped garlic, then reduce the heat slightly and simmer gently for 7–10 minutes, stirring occassionally, or until the couscous is just tender. Serve piping hot, ladled into individual serving bowls.

Energy 130kcal/541kJ; Protein 2.6g; Carbohydrate 21.3g, of which sugars 3.9g; Fat 4.3g, of which saturates 0.6g; Cholesterol 0mg; Calcium 19mg; Fibre 1.3g; Sodium 11mg.

SPINACH AND RISOTTO RICE SOUP

USE VERY FRESH, YOUNG SPINACH LEAVES TO PREPARE THIS LIGHT AND FRESH-TASTING SOUP. RISOTTO RICE HAS A SOFT, CREAMY TEXTURE WHICH HELPS TO MAKE A VELVETY, SATISFYING SOUP.

SERVES FOUR

INGREDIENTS
675g/1½lb fresh spinach, washed
45ml/3 tbsp extra virgin olive oil
1 small onion, finely chopped
2 garlic cloves, finely chopped
1 small fresh red chilli, seeded and
   finely chopped
115g/4oz/generous 1 cup risotto rice
1.2 litres/2 pints/5 cups
   vegetable stock
60ml/4 tbsp grated Pecorino cheese
salt and ground black pepper

1 Place the spinach in a large pan with just the water that clings to its leaves after washing. Add a large pinch of salt. Heat gently until the spinach has wilted, then remove from the heat and drain, reserving any liquid.

2 Either chop the spinach finely using a large knife or place in a food processor and process to a fairly coarse purée.

3 Heat the oil in a large pan and gently cook the onion, garlic and chilli for 4–5 minutes until softened. Stir in the rice until well coated, then pour in the stock and reserved spinach liquid. Bring to the boil, lower the heat and simmer for 10 minutes.

4 Add the spinach, with salt and pepper to taste. Cook for 5–7 minutes more, until the rice is tender. Check the seasoning and serve with the Pecorino cheese.

Energy 279kcal/1157kJ; Protein 11.4g; Carbohydrate 25.9g, of which sugars 2.5g; Fat 14.2g, of which saturates 4.4g; Cholesterol 15mg; Calcium 381mg; Fibre 2.6g; Sodium 322mg.

BEEF AND BARLEY SOUP

THIS FARMHOUSE SOUP, COMBINING BARLEY, SPLIT PEAS AND BEEF, MAKES A TRULY RESTORATIVE DISH FOR A COLD DAY. LIKE A GOOD STEW, THE FLAVOUR DEVELOPS BEST IF IT IS MADE A DAY IN ADVANCE.

2 Meanwhile, trim any fat or gristle from the meat and cut into small pieces. Chop the remaining onions finely. Drain the stock from the bones, make it up with water to 2 litres/3½ pints/9 cups, and return to the rinsed pan with the meat, onions, barley and split peas.

3 Season, bring to the boil, and skim if necessary. Reduce the heat, cover and simmer for about 30 minutes.

4 Add the rest of the vegetables and simmer for 1 hour, or until the meat is tender. Check the seasoning. Serve in large warmed bowls, generously sprinkled with parsley.

COOK'S TIP
Other grains and beans can be used in this soup. Try cannellini or haricot beans combined with freekah or spelt grains.

SERVES SIX TO EIGHT

INGREDIENTS
   450–675g/1–1½lb rib steak, on
      the bone
   2 large onions
   50g/2oz/¼ cup pearl barley
   50g/2oz/¼ cup green split peas
   3 large carrots, chopped
   2 white turnips, chopped
   3 celery stalks, chopped
   1 large or 2 medium leeks,
      thinly sliced
   sea salt and ground black pepper
   chopped fresh parsley, to serve

1 Bone the meat, put the bones and half an onion, roughly sliced, into a large pan. Cover with cold water, season and bring to the boil. Skim, then simmer for 1–1½ hours, until required.

Energy 194kcal/814kJ; Protein 16.7g; Carbohydrate 19.6g, of which sugars 9g; Fat 6g, of which saturates 2.2g; Cholesterol 33mg; Calcium 62mg; Fibre 3.9g; Sodium 61mg.

CHICKEN, LEEK AND BARLEY SOUP

THIS RECIPE IS BASED ON THE TRADITIONAL SCOTTISH SOUP, COCK-A-LEEKIE. THE UNUSUAL COMBINATION OF LEEKS AND PRUNES IS SURPRISINGLY DELICIOUS, AND PEARL BARLEY ADDS BODY.

SERVES SIX

INGREDIENTS
115g/4oz/²⁄₃ cup pearl barley
1 chicken, weighing about 2kg/4¹⁄₄lb
900g/2lb leeks
1 fresh bay leaf
a few fresh parsley stalks and
  thyme sprigs
1 large carrot, thickly sliced
2.4 litres/4 pints/10 cups chicken
  or beef stock
400g/14oz ready-to-eat prunes
salt and ground black pepper
chopped fresh parsley, to garnish

1 Rinse the pearl barley thoroughly in a sieve under cold running water, then cook it in a large pan of boiling water for about 10 minutes. Drain the barley, rinse well again and drain thoroughly. Set aside in a cool place.

2 Cut the breast portions off the chicken and set aside, then place the remaining chicken carcass in the pan. Cut half the leeks into 5cm/2in lengths and add them to the pan. Tie the herbs together into a bouquet garni and add to the pan with the carrot and stock.

3 Bring the stock to the boil, then reduce the heat and cover the pan. Simmer gently for 1 hour. Skim off any scum when the water first starts to boil and occasionally during simmering.

4 Add the chicken breasts to the pan and continue to cook for another 30 minutes until they are just cooked. Leave until cool enough to handle.

5 Strain the stock. Reserve the chicken breast portions and the meat from the carcass. Discard all the skin, bones, cooked vegetables and herbs. Skim as much fat as you can from the stock, then return it to the pan.

6 Add the pearl barley to the stock. Bring to the boil over a medium heat, then lower the heat and cook very gently for 15–20 minutes, until the barley is just cooked and tender. Season the soup with 5ml/1 tsp each salt and ground black pepper.

7 Add the ready-to-eat prunes to the pan, then thinly slice the remaining leeks and add them to the pan. Bring to the boil, then cover the pan and simmer gently for about 10 minutes, or until the leeks are just cooked.

8 Slice the chicken breast portions and then add them to the soup with the remaining chicken meat from the carcass, sliced or cut into neat pieces. Reheat the soup, if necessary, then ladle it into warm, deep soup plates and sprinkle with plenty of chopped parsley to garnish.

Energy 326kcal/1383kJ; Protein 33.7g; Carbohydrate 44.4g, of which sugars 27.2g; Fat 2.7g, of which saturates 0.5g; Cholesterol 82mg; Calcium 73mg; Fibre 7.5g; Sodium 85mg.

SPICY COUSCOUS AND SHELLFISH BROTH

SOME COUSCOUS DISHES INCLUDE A SOUP-LIKE STEW, WHICH IS LADLED OVER THE COOKED COUSCOUS AND MOPPED UP WITH LOTS OF BREAD. THE RESULTING MEAL IS WARMING AND DELICIOUS.

SERVES FOUR TO SIX

INGREDIENTS
500g/1¼lb/3 cups medium couscous
5ml/1 tsp salt
600ml/1 pint/2½ cups warm water
45ml/3 tbsp sunflower oil
5–10ml/1–2 tsp harissa
75g/3oz/6 tbsp butter
500g/1¼lb mussels in their shells,
   scrubbed, with beards removed
500g/1¼lb uncooked prawns
   (shrimp) in their shells
juice of 1 lemon
2 shallots, finely chopped
5ml/1 tsp coriander seeds, roasted
   and ground
5ml/1 tsp cumin seeds, roasted
   and ground
2.5ml/½ tsp ground turmeric
2.5ml/½ tsp cayenne pepper
5–10ml/1–2 tsp plain (all-purpose)
   flour
600ml/1 pint/2½ cups fish stock
120ml/4fl oz/½ cup double
   (heavy) cream
salt and ground black pepper
small bunch of fresh coriander
   (cilantro), finely chopped, to serve

1 Preheat the oven to 180°C/350°F/Gas 4. Place the couscous in a bowl. Stir the salt into the water, then pour over the couscous, stirring. Set aside for 10 minutes.

2 Stir the sunflower oil into the harissa to make a paste, then, using your fingers, rub it into the couscous and break up any lumps. Tip into an ovenproof dish. Dice 25g/1oz/2 tbsp of the butter and dot it over the couscous. Cover with foil and heat in the oven for about 20 minutes.

3 Meanwhile, put the mussels and prawns in a pan, add the lemon juice and 50ml/2fl oz/¼ cup water, cover and cook for 3–4 minutes, shaking the pan, until the mussels have opened. Drain the shellfish, reserving the liquor, and shell about two-thirds of the mussels and prawns. Discard any closed mussels.

4 Heat the remaining butter in a large pan. Cook the shallots for 5 minutes, or until softened. Add the spices and fry for 1 minute. Off the heat, stir in the flour, the fish stock and shellfish cooking liquor. Bring to the boil, stirring. Add the cream and simmer, stirring occasionally, for about 10 minutes. Season with salt and pepper, add the shellfish and most of the fresh coriander. Heat through, then sprinkle with the remaining coriander.

5 Fluff up the couscous with a fork or your fingers, working in the melted butter. To serve, pass round the couscous and ladle the broth over the top.

COOK'S TIP
Eaten on its own, couscous has a bland flavour, but readily absorbs the flavours of other foods, making it a good, filling base for many dishes.

Energy 496kcal/2062kJ; Protein 17.2g; Carbohydrate 45.5g, of which sugars 1.2g; Fat 28.3g, of which saturates 14g; Cholesterol 152mg; Calcium 134mg; Fibre 0.6g; Sodium 636mg.

UDON NOODLE SOUP

THIS INVIGORATING JAPANESE-STYLE SOUP IS FLAVOURED WITH JUST A HINT OF CHILLI AND SOYA
BEAN PASTE. UDON ARE ROUND NOODLES MADE FROM WHEAT FLOUR AND WATER.

SERVES FOUR

INGREDIENTS

   1 litre/1¾ pints/4 cups water
   45ml/3 tbsp mugi miso (bean paste)
   200g/7oz/2 scant cups udon noodles
    or soba noodles
   30ml/2 tbsp sake or dry sherry
   15ml/1 tbsp rice or wine vinegar
   45ml/3 tbsp Japanese soy sauce
   115g/4oz asparagus tips or
    mangetouts (snowpeas), thinly
    sliced diagonally
   50g/2oz/scant 1 cup shiitake
    mushrooms, stalks removed and
    thinly sliced
   1 carrot, sliced into julienne strips
   3 spring onions (scallions), thinly
    sliced diagonally
   5ml/1 tsp dried chilli flakes, to serve
salt and ground black pepper

1 Bring the water to the boil in a pan. Pour 150ml/¼ pint/⅔ cup of the boiling water over the miso and stir until dissolved, then set aside.

2 Meanwhile, bring another large pan of lightly salted water to the boil, add the noodles and cook according to the packet instructions until just tender.

3 Drain the noodles in a colander. Rinse under cold running water, then drain again.

COOK'S TIP
Miso is a thick paste made from soya beans combined with barley, rice or wheat. It ranges in colour and depth of flavour, from light and sweet to strong, and dark.

4 Add the sake or sherry, rice or wine vinegar and soy sauce to the pan of boiling water. Boil gently for 3 minutes or until the alcohol has evaporated, then reduce the heat and stir in the miso mixture. Add the asparagus or mangetouts, mushrooms, carrot and spring onions, and simmer for 2 minutes until the vegetables are just tender. Season to taste.

Energy 254kcal/1076kJ; Protein 10.2g; Carbohydrate 48.1g, of which sugars 4.9g; Fat 3.6g, of which saturates 0.1g; Cholesterol 0mg; Calcium 37mg; Fibre 3.4g; Sodium 814mg.

POLENTA FRITTERS

Two rounds of polenta are sandwiched together with a filling of rosemary, tomatoes and Italian cheeses, then fried to make a delicious appetizer or light lunch.

SERVES SIX

INGREDIENTS

250g/9oz/1½ cups polenta
30–45ml/2–3 tbsp tomato
  purée (paste)
30–45ml/2–3 tbsp diced ripe fresh or
  canned chopped tomatoes
30ml/2 tbsp chopped fresh rosemary
30–45ml/2–3 tbsp freshly grated
  Parmesan or Pecorino cheese
130g/4½oz mozzarella, Gorgonzola
  or Fontina cheese, finely chopped
half vegetable and half olive oil,
  for deep-frying
1–2 eggs, lightly beaten
plain (all-purpose) flour, for dusting
salt
diced red (bell) pepper, shredded
  lettuce and rosemary sprigs, to garnish

COOK'S TIPS
• If the polenta is too thin the fritters will fall apart; if too thick they will be heavy.
• Do not use instant polenta as the sandwiches will fall apart on cooking.
• The fritters can be cooked ahead of time and reheated in the oven at 200°C/400°F/Gas 6 for 5–10 minutes.

1 In a large pan, combine the polenta with 250ml/8fl oz/1 cup cold water and stir. Add 750ml/1¼ pints/3 cups boiling water and cook, stirring constantly, for about 30 minutes until the mixture is very thick and no longer grainy. If the mixture is thick but still not cooked through, stir in a little more boiling water and simmer until soft. Season.

2 Pour the mixture into an oiled baking dish, forming a layer about 1cm/½in thick. Lightly cover, then cool and chill.

3 Using a 6–7.5cm/2½–3in plain pastry (cookie) cutter or the rim of a glass, cut the polenta into rounds.

4 In a small bowl, combine the tomato purée with the diced tomatoes. Spread a little of the mixture on the soft, moist side of a polenta round, sprinkle with rosemary and a little of the grated and chopped cheeses, then top with another round of polenta, the moist soft side against the filling. Press the edges together to seal the sandwiches. Fill the remaining polenta rounds in the same way.

5 Heat the oil in a wide, deep frying pan, to a depth of about 5cm/2in, until it is hot enough to brown a cube of bread in 30 seconds.

6 Dip a sandwich into the beaten egg, then coat in the flour. Gently lower it into the hot oil and fry for 4–5 minutes, turning once. Drain on kitchen paper. Cook the remaining polenta sandwiches in the same way. Serve warm, garnished with pepper, lettuce and rosemary.

COOK'S TIP
Polenta makes the basis of a very filling meal. Serve with a light salad for a lunchtime dish or appetizer.

Energy 136Kcal/573kJ; Protein 9.8g; Carbohydrate 16g, of which sugars 0.9g; Fat 4.1g, of which saturates 2.6g; Cholesterol 13mg; Calcium 34mg; Fibre 1.4g; Sodium 97mg.

CORN FRITTERS

SOMETIMES IT IS THE SIMPLEST OF DISHES THAT TASTES THE BEST. THESE FRITTERS, PACKED WITH CRUNCHY CORN, ARE VERY EASY TO PREPARE AND UNDERSTANDABLY POPULAR.

MAKES TWELVE

INGREDIENTS

3 corn cobs, total weight about 250g/9oz
1 garlic clove, crushed
small bunch fresh coriander (cilantro), chopped
1 small fresh red or green chilli, seeded and finely chopped
1 spring onion (scallion), finely chopped
15ml/1 tbsp soy sauce
75g/3oz/¾ cup rice flour or plain (all-purpose) flour
2 eggs, lightly beaten
60ml/4 tbsp water
oil, for shallow frying
salt and ground black pepper
sweet chilli sauce, to serve

1 Using a sharp knife, slice the kernels from the cobs and place them in a large bowl. Add the garlic, chopped coriander, red or green chilli, spring onion, soy sauce, flour, beaten eggs and water and mix well. Season with salt and pepper to taste and mix again. The mixture should be firm enough to hold its shape, but not stiff.

2 Heat the oil in a large frying pan. Add spoonfuls of the corn mixture, gently spreading each one out with the back of the spoon to make a roundish fritter. Cook for 1–2 minutes on each side.

3 Drain on kitchen paper and keep hot while frying more fritters in the same way. Serve hot with sweet chilli sauce.

Energy 106kcal/443kJ; Protein 2.3g; Carbohydrate 7.4g, of which sugars 0.5g; Fat 7.8g, of which saturates 1.1g; Cholesterol 32mg; Calcium 22mg; Fibre 0.7g; Sodium 13mg.

RICE AND VEGETABLE FRITTERS

BROWN RICE GIVES THESE FRITTERS A DELICIOUS NUTTY FLAVOUR AND TEXTURE, AND IT IS
ALSO A GOOD SOURCE OF B VITAMINS AND FIBRE. THE FRITTERS ARE A CREATIVE WAY TO USE UP ANY
LEFTOVER RICE, AND THEY MAKE A COLOURFUL VEGETARIAN APPETIZER.

<u>MAKES SIXTEEN</u>

INGREDIENTS
    200g/7oz cold cooked brown rice
    4 spring onions (scallions), chopped
    1 red (bell) pepper, diced
    2 garlic cloves, crushed
    60ml/4 tbsp freshly grated Parmesan
    1 large egg, lightly beaten
    60ml/4 tbsp double (heavy) cream
    60ml/4 tbsp plain (all-purpose) flour
    vegetable oil, for frying
    salt and ground black pepper

1 Mix together the cooked rice, spring onions, red pepper, garlic, Parmesan, egg, cream, flour and seasoning in a bowl to make a sloppy batter.

2 Heat enough oil to lightly coat the bottom of a frying pan. Place two heaped dessertspoons of the rice mixture into the hot oil and flatten the top slightly with a spatula.

3 Cook the fritters in batches for 3 minutes each side until golden and set. Drain on crumpled kitchen paper and keep warm while you cook the remaining mixture.

COOK'S TIP
Spicy mango chutney or sweet chilli sauce work well with these fritters.

Energy 92kcal/385kJ; Protein 2.9g; Carbohydrate 8.7g, of which sugars 0.9g; Fat 5.3g, of which saturates 1.4g; Cholesterol 18mg; Calcium 57mg; Fibre 0.5g; Sodium 47mg.

CORNMEAL BAKED WITH CHEESE

CORNMEAL IS FIRST COOKED TO A PORRIDGE-LIKE CONSISTENCY, THEN BAKED WITH FETA AND A STRONG CHEESE TO GIVE IT A PLENTY OF FLAVOUR. THIS BAKE IS SUBSTANTIAL, SO SERVE IT IN SMALL WEDGES WITH A HERB SALAD AND FRESH TOMATO SALSA TO MAKE AN IDEAL STARTER.

SERVES FOUR TO SIX

INGREDIENTS

130g/4½oz/generous 1 cup coarse ground cornmeal
1 litre/1¾ pints/4 cups water
50g/2oz/4 tbsp unsalted (sweet) butter
350g/12oz/1½ cups feta cheese, drained and crumbled
50g/2oz/½ cup grated strong, hard cheese (such as Cheddar), for sprinkling
salt and ground black pepper
grilled bacon and spring onions (scallions), sliced lengthways, to garnish
tomato sauce, to serve

1 Preheat the oven to 190°C/375°F/ Gas 5. Stirring occasionally, dry-fry the cornmeal in a large pan for 3–4 minutes, or until it changes colour. Remove from the heat.

2 Slowly pour in the water and add a little salt. Return the pan to the heat and stir well until the cornmeal thickens a little. Cover, reduce the heat and leave to cook for 25 minutes, stirring often.

COOK'S TIP
Cornmeal has a mild flavour and blends well with ingredients with a more powerful taste. You can use other types of cheese in this recipe.

3 Remove from the heat when thick enough to hold a wide trail when a wooden spoon is lifted from the mixture. Stir in the butter and feta cheese and season well.

4 Spoon into a 20cm/8in greased springform tin (pan). Bake for 25–30 minutes or until firm. Leave overnight or for 2–3 hours. Serve sprinkled with cheese, bacon and spring onions, with tomato salsa.

Energy 322kcal/1337kJ; Protein 13.3g; Carbohydrate 16.8g, of which sugars 0.9g; Fat 22.1g, of which saturates 14.1g; Cholesterol 67mg; Calcium 274mg; Fibre 0.5g; Sodium 951mg.

SPICED NOODLE PANCAKES

THE DELICATE RICE NOODLES PUFF UP IN THE HOT OIL TO GIVE A SUPERB, CRUNCHY BITE THAT JUST MELTS IN THE MOUTH. FOR MAXIMUM ENJOYMENT, SERVE THE GOLDEN PANCAKES AS SOON AS THEY ARE COOKED AND SAVOUR THE SUBTLE BLEND OF SPICES AND WONDERFULLY CRISP TEXTURE.

SERVES FOUR

INGREDIENTS
    150g/5oz dried vermicelli rice
      noodles
    1 red chilli, finely diced
    10ml/2 tsp garlic salt
    5ml/1 tsp ground ginger
    ¼ small red onion, very finely diced
    5ml/1 tsp finely chopped lemon grass
    5ml/1 tsp ground cumin
    5ml/1 tsp ground coriander
    large pinch of ground turmeric
    salt
    vegetable oil, for frying
    bottled sweet chilli sauce, for dipping

1 Roughly break up the noodles and place in a large bowl. Pour over enough boiling water to cover and soak for 4–5 minutes. Drain and rinse under cold water. Dry on kitchen paper.

2 Transfer the noodles to a bowl and add the chilli, garlic salt, ground ginger, red onion, lemon grass, ground cumin, coriander and turmeric. Toss well to mix and season with salt.

3 Heat 5–6cm/2–2½in oil in a wok. Working in batches, drop tablespoons of the noodle mixture into the oil. Flatten using the back of a skimmer or metal spatula and cook for 1–2 minutes on each side until crisp and golden.

4 Drain on kitchen paper and serve with the chilli sauce.

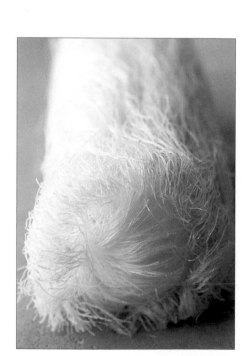

Energy 248kcal/1031kJ; Protein 2.4g; Carbohydrate 32.7g, of which sugars 0.9g; Fat 11.5g, of which saturates 1.3g; Cholesterol 0mg; Calcium 32mg; Fibre 1.1g; Sodium 22mg.

TORTILLA WRAP WITH TABBOULEH

TO BE SUCCESSFUL THIS CLASSIC MIDDLE EASTERN BULGUR WHEAT SALAD NEEDS SPRING ONIONS, LEMON JUICE, PLENTY OF FRESH HERBS AND LOTS OF FRESHLY GROUND BLACK PEPPER. WAIT FOR THE FLAVOURSOME, SUN-RIPENED SUMMER CROP OF AVOCADOES FOR THE VERY BEST RESULTS.

3 Add the mint, parsley, spring onions and cucumber to the bulgur wheat and mix thoroughly. Blend together the olive oil and lemon juice and pour over the tabbouleh, season to taste and toss well to mix. Chill for 30 minutes to allow the flavours to mingle.

4 To make the guacamole, place the avocado in a bowl and add the lemon juice, chilli and garlic. Season to taste and mash with a fork to form a smooth purée. Stir in the red pepper.

SERVES FOUR TO SIX

INGREDIENTS
    175g/6oz/1 cup bulgur wheat
    30ml/3 tbsp chopped fresh mint
    30ml/3 tbsp chopped fresh flat
      leaf parsley
    1 bunch spring onions (scallions)
      (about 6), sliced
    ½ cucumber, diced
    50ml/2fl oz/¼ cup extra virgin
      olive oil
    juice of 1 large lemon
    salt and ground black pepper
    flat leaf parsley, to garnish (optional)
    4 wheat tortillas, to serve
For the guacamole
    1 ripe avocado, stoned (pitted),
      peeled and diced
    juice of ½ lemon
    ½ red chilli, seeded and sliced
    1 garlic clove, crushed
    ½ red (bell) pepper, seeded and
      finely diced

1 To make the tabbouleh, place the bulgur wheat in a large heatproof bowl and pour over enough boiling water to cover.

2 Leave for 30 minutes until the grains are tender but still retain a little resistance to the bite. Drain thoroughly in a sieve, then tip back into the bowl.

5 Warm the tortillas in a dry frying pan and serve either flat, folded or rolled up with the tabbouleh and guacamole. Garnish with parsley, if using.

COOK'S TIP
The soaking time for bulgur wheat can vary. For the best results, follow the instructions on the packet and taste the grain every now and again to check whether it is tender enough.

Energy 259kcal/1081kJ; Protein 5.1g; Carbohydrate 35g, of which sugars 1.9g; Fat 11.5g, of which saturates 1.9g; Cholesterol 0mg; Calcium 55mg; Fibre 1.7g; Sodium 52mg.

STUFFED VINE LEAVES

VINE LEAVES STUFFED WITH TENDER, SEASONED RICE ARE A CLASSIC GREEK MEZE DISH. THIS VERSION HAS A FLAVOURSOME COMBINATION OF RICE, HERBS, YELLOW SPLIT PEAS AND LAMB.

SERVES FOUR TO SIX

INGREDIENTS
  250g/9oz vine leaves
  30ml/2 tbsp olive oil
  1 large onion, finely chopped
  250g/9oz minced (ground) lamb
  50g/2oz/¼ cup yellow split peas
  75g/3oz/½ cup cooked rice
  30ml/2 tbsp chopped fresh parsley
  30ml/2 tbsp chopped fresh mint
  30ml/2 tbsp chopped fresh chives
  3–4 spring onions (scallions),
    finely chopped
  juice of 2 lemons
  30ml/2 tbsp tomato purée (paste)
  30ml/2 tbsp sugar
  salt and ground black pepper
  yogurt and pitta bread, to serve

1 Blanch fresh vine leaves, if using, in boiling water for 1–2 minutes to soften them, or rinse preserved, bottled or canned vine leaves under cold water.

2 Heat the olive oil in a large frying pan and fry the onion for a few minutes until slightly softened. Add the minced lamb and fry over a medium heat until well browned, stirring frequently. Season with salt and pepper and remove from the heat.

3 Place the split peas in a small pan with enough water to cover and bring to the boil. Cover the pan and simmer gently over a low heat for 12–15 minutes, until soft. Drain the split peas if necessary.

4 Stir the split peas, cooked rice, chopped herbs, spring onions, and the juice of one of the lemons into the meat. Add the tomato purée and then knead until thoroughly blended.

5 Place each vine leaf on a chopping board with the vein side up. Place 15ml/1 tbsp of the meat mixture on each leaf and fold the stem end over the meat. Fold the sides in towards the centre and then roll into a neat parcel.

6 Line the base of a large pan with unstuffed leaves and arrange the rolled leaves in layers on top. Stir the remaining lemon juice and sugar into 150ml/¼ pint/⅔ cup water and pour over the leaves. Place a heatproof plate over the stuffed vine leaves.

7 Cover the pan and cook over a very low heat for 2 hours, checking occasionally and adding extra water if necessary. Serve with yogurt and bread.

COOK'S TIP
If using preserved vine leaves, soak them overnight in cold water and then rinse several times before use.

Energy 319Kcal/1336kJ; Protein 18.4g; Carbohydrate 29.8g, of which sugars 16.2g; Fat 14.8g, of which saturates 4.8g; Cholesterol 48mg; Calcium 117mg; Fibre 4.2g; Sodium 98mg.

POLENTA CHIP DIPPERS

THESE TASTY PARMESAN-FLAVOURED BATONS ARE MADE USING INSTANT POLENTA WHICH COOKS FASTER THAN OTHER TYPES OF CORNMEAL. THEY ARE BEST SERVED WARM FROM THE OVEN WITH A SPICY DIP.

MAKES ABOUT EIGHTY

INGREDIENTS
  1.5 litres/2½ pints/6¼ cups water
  10ml/2 tsp salt
  375g/13oz/3¼ cups instant polenta
  150g/5oz/1½ cups freshly grated
  Parmesan cheese
  90g/3½oz/scant ½ cup butter
  10ml/2 tsp cracked black pepper
  olive oil, for brushing
  salt

1 Pour the water into a large heavy pan and bring to the boil over a high heat. Reduce the heat, add the salt and pour in the polenta in a steady stream, stirring constantly with a wooden spoon. Cook over a low heat, stirring constantly, until the mixture thickens and starts to come away from the sides of the pan – this will take about 5 minutes.

2 Remove the pan from the heat and add the cheese, butter, pepper and salt to taste. Stir well until the butter has completely melted and the mixture is smooth.

3 Pour on to a smooth surface, such as a marble slab or a baking sheet. Spread the polenta out using a palette knife (metal spatula) to a thickness of 2cm/¾in and shape into a rectangle. Leave for at least 30 minutes to become quite cold. Meanwhile preheat the oven to 200°C/400°F/Gas 6 and lightly oil two or three baking sheets with some olive oil.

COOK'S TIP
The unbaked dough can be made a day ahead, then wrapped in clear film (plastic wrap) and kept in the refrigerator until ready to bake.

4 Cut the polenta slab in half, then carefully cut into even-size strips using a sharp knife.

5 Bake the polenta chips for about 40–50 minutes until they are dark golden brown and crunchy. Turn them over from time to time during cooking. Serve warm.

Energy 39kcal/162kJ; Protein 1.2g; Carbohydrate 3.4g, of which sugars 0g; Fat 2.2g, of which saturates 1g; Cholesterol 4mg; Calcium 23mg; Fibre 0.1g; Sodium 76mg.

MAMALIGA BALLS

THE MAMALIGA BALLS IN THIS RECIPE CONTAIN BITE-SIZED PIECES OF SALAMI, BUT CHUNKS OF SMOKED HAM OR CHEESE ARE EQUALLY SUITABLE. MAMALIGA IS A THICK CORNMEAL PORRIDGE-LIKE DISH WHICH CAN BE SERVED PLAIN OR TURNED INTO BALLS, AS HERE.

SERVES SIX TO EIGHT

INGREDIENTS
250g/9oz/generous 2 cups fine
  cornmeal
600ml/1 pint/2½ cups lightly
  salted water
generous knob (pat) of butter
115g/4oz/1 cup salami,
  roughly chopped
vegetable oil, for deep-frying
pan-fried tomatoes and fresh herbs,
  to serve

1 Stir the cornmeal and water together in a heavy pan. Bring to the boil and, stirring continuously, cook for 12 minutes, or until suitable for rolling into balls. Stir in the butter.

VARIATION
Try stuffing the mamaliga balls with cheese or other strong-flavoured fillings instead of the salami.

2 When cool, with lightly floured hands, roll the mixture into balls double the size of a walnut. Press a piece of salami into the middle and neatly roll again.

3 Heat the oil to 180–190°C/ 350–375°F and fry the balls for 2–3 minutes or until golden brown. Drain well on kitchen paper. Serve with fried tomatoes and chopped herbs.

Energy 246kcal/1022kJ; Protein 6g; Carbohydrate 22.9g, of which sugars 0.1g; Fat 14.2g, of which saturates 4g; Cholesterol 17mg; Calcium 3mg; Fibre 0.7g; Sodium 274mg.

STEAMED RICE BALLS WITH SPICY SAUCE

BITESIZE BALLS OF STEAMED PORK AND MUSHROOMS ROLLED IN JASMINE RICE MAKE ELEGANT CANAPÉS TO SERVE WITH PRE-DINNER DRINKS, OR FOR A STARTER YOU COULD SERVE THEM AS PART OF A SELECTION OF DIM SUM. THE DIPPING SAUCE HAS A SWEET-AND-SOUR FLAVOUR.

SERVES FOUR

INGREDIENTS
  30ml/2 tbsp oil
  200g/7oz/scant 3 cups finely
    chopped shiitake mushrooms
  400g/14oz minced (ground) pork
  4 spring onions (scallions), chopped
  2 garlic cloves, crushed
  15ml/1 tbsp fish sauce
  15ml/1 tbsp soy sauce
  15ml/1 tsp grated fresh root ginger
  60ml/4 tbsp finely chopped
    coriander (cilantro)
  1 egg, lightly beaten
  salt and ground black pepper
  200g/7oz/1 cup jasmine rice
For the dipping sauce
  120ml/4fl oz/½ cup sweet
    chilli sauce
  105ml/7 tbsp soy sauce
  15ml/1 tbsp Chinese rice wine
  5–10ml/1–2 tsp chilli oil

2 To cook, place the rice in a bowl. With wet hands, divide the mushroom mixture into 20 portions and roll each one into a firm ball. Roll each ball in the rice then arrange the balls, spaced apart, in two baking parchment-lined tiers of a bamboo steamer.

3 Cover the steamer and place over a wok of simmering water. Steam for 1 hour 15 minutes. (Check the water often, replenishing when necessary.)

4 Meanwhile, combine all the dipping sauce ingredients in a small bowl.

5 When the balls are cooked, remove from the steamer and serve warm or at room temperature with the bowl of spicy dipping sauce.

1 Heat the oil in a large wok, then add the mushrooms and stir-fry over a high heat for 2–3 minutes. Transfer to a food processor with the pork, spring onions, garlic, fish sauce, soy sauce, ginger, coriander and beaten egg. Process for 30–40 seconds, transfer to a bowl and combine well by hand. Cover and chill in the refrigerator for 3–4 hours or overnight.

COOK'S TIP
Jasmine rice has a soft, sticky texture that forms a casing around these Thai-style balls. You could also try sushi rice.

Energy 428kcal/1790kJ; Protein 28.9g; Carbohydrate 50.1g, of which sugars 9.7g; Fat 12.4g, of which saturates 2.7g; Cholesterol 111mg; Calcium 61mg; Fibre 1.6g; Sodium 1296mg.

SMOKED TROUT ON RYE WITH BEETROOT

THIS DELICIOUS APPETIZER IS MADE OF INGREDIENTS THAT EACH HAVE STRONG AND DISTINCTIVE FLAVOURS YET WORK TOGETHER BRILLIANTLY WELL. THE FIRM TEXTURE OF RYE BREAD IS A GOOD FOIL FOR THE LIGHT TOPPING. FOR CANAPES SIMPLY CUT THE BREAD INTO BITESIZED PIECES.

SERVES FOUR

INGREDIENTS

   30ml/2 tbsp horseradish sauce
   15ml/1 tbsp sour cream
   2 cooked beetroots (beets) (not in
     vinegar), diced
   4 smoked trout fillets,
     halved crossways
   4 slices rye bread, halved crossways
   salt and ground black pepper
   wedges of lemon, to serve

1 To make the beetroot cream, mix together the horseradish sauce and sour cream, season and gently stir in the beetroot.

2 Arrange the trout fillets on the slices of rye bread, top with a spoonful of the beetroot cream and a sprig of dill. Serve with wedges of lemon.

Energy 193kcal/812kJ; Protein 22.1g; Carbohydrate 14.4g, of which sugars 3g; Fat 5.6g, of which saturates 0.6g; Cholesterol 3mg; Calcium 40mg; Fibre 1.7g; Sodium 283mg.

SIMPLE ROLLED SUSHI

MAKING THESE SIMPLE ROLLS IS AN EXCELLENT WAY OF LEARNING THE ART OF ROLLING SUSHI.
JAPANESE SUSHI RICE STICKS TOGETHER WHEN COOKED DUE TO ITS HIGH STARCH CONTENT. THIS
QUALITY MAKES IT PERFECT FOR ROLLING. YOU WILL NEED A BAMBOO MAT FOR THE PROCESS.

MAKES 12 ROLLS OR 72 SLICES

INGREDIENTS
 400g/14oz/2 cups sushi rice, soaked
  for 20 minutes in water to cover
 55ml/3½ tbsp rice vinegar
 15ml/1 tbsp sugar
 2.5ml/½ tsp salt
 6 sheets yaki-nori seaweed
 200g/7oz tuna, in one piece
 200g/7oz salmon, in one piece
 wasabi paste
 ½ cucumber, quartered lengthways
  and seeded
 pickled ginger, to garnish (optional)
 Japanese soy sauce, to serve

1 Drain the rice, then put in a pan with 525ml/18fl oz/2¼ cups water. Bring to the boil, then lower the heat, cover and simmer for 20 minutes, or until all the liquid has been absorbed. Meanwhile, heat the vinegar, sugar and salt, stir well and cool. Add to the hot rice, then remove the pan from the heat and allow to stand (covered) for 20 minutes.

2 Cut the yaki-nori sheets in half lengthways. Cut each of the tuna and salmon into four long sticks, about the same length as the long side of the yaki-nori, and about 1cm/½in square if viewed from the end.

3 Place a sheet of yaki-nori, shiny side down, on a bamboo mat. Divide the rice into 12 portions. Spread one portion over the yaki-nori, leaving a 1cm/½in clear space at the top and bottom.

4 Spread a little wasabi paste in a horizontal line along the middle of the rice and place one or two sticks of tuna on this.

5 Holding the mat and the edge of the yaki-nori nearest to you, roll up the yaki-nori and rice into a cylinder with the tuna in the middle. Use the mat as a guide – do not roll it into the food. Roll the rice tightly so that it sticks together and encloses the filling firmly.

6 Carefully roll the sushi off the mat. Make 11 more rolls in the same way, four for each filling ingredient, but do not use wasabi with the cucumber. Use a wet knife to cut each roll into six slices and stand them on a platter. Garnish with pickled ginger, if you wish, and serve with soy sauce.

Energy 31kcal/128kJ; Protein 1.7g; Carbohydrate 4.8g, of which sugars 0.3g; Fat 0.5g, of which saturates 0.1g; Cholesterol 2mg; Calcium 4mg; Fibre 0.1g; Sodium 3mg.

SALADS
AND SIDES

Rice, couscous and polenta are some of
the classic grain accompaniments that go so well
with main dishes. What is striking about this
chapter is the variety of side dishes and salads
that can be made using grains. For example,
look out for North African-inspired Tofu and
Wild Rice Salad or exotic Quinoa Salad with
Mango. Grains add both substance and
nutritional value to salads, and many of these
dishes could make satisfying main courses.

QUINOA SALAD <u>WITH</u> MANGO

SINCE QUINOA HAS A MILD, SLIGHTLY BITTER TASTE, IT IS BEST COMBINED WITH INGREDIENTS THAT HAVE A MORE ROBUST FLAVOUR, SUCH AS FRESH HERBS, CHILLI, FRUIT AND NUTS, AS IN THIS SUPER-HEALTHY SALAD. THIS WOULD WORK VERY WELL SERVED WITH SLICES OF GRIDDLED HALLOUMI CHEESE.

SERVES FOUR

INGREDIENTS
  130g/4½ oz quinoa
  1 mango
  60ml/4 tbsp pine nuts
  large handful fresh basil,
    roughly chopped
  large handful fresh flat leaf parsley,
    roughly chopped
  large handful fresh mint,
    roughly chopped
  1 mild long fresh red chilli, seeded
    and chopped
For the dressing
  1 tbsp lemon juice
  1 tbsp extra virgin olive oil
  salt and ground black pepper

1 Put the quinoa in a pan and cover with cold water. Season with salt and bring to the boil. Reduce the heat, cover the pan with a lid and simmer for 12 minutes or until the quinoa is tender. Drain well.

2 Meanwhile, prepare the mango. Cut vertically down each side of the stone (pit). Taking the two large slices, cut the flesh into a criss-cross pattern down to (but not through) the skin.

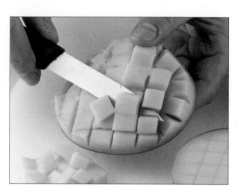

3 Press each half inside out, then cut the mango cubes away from the skin.

4 Toast the pine nuts for a few minutes in a dry frying pan until golden, then remove from the heat.

5 Mix together the ingredients for the dressing and season well.

6 Put the cooked quinoa into a bowl and add the herbs and chilli. Pour the dressing into the bowl and fork lightly until combined. Season to taste and transfer to a bowl or four shallow dishes. Arrange the mango on top of the herby quinoa and sprinkle with the pine nuts.

Energy 206kcal/857kJ; Protein 4.5g; Carbohydrate 23.1g, of which sugars 6.2g; Fat 11.2g, of which saturates 1g; Cholesterol 0mg; Calcium 62mg; Fibre 2.5g; Sodium 9mg.

COUSCOUS SALAD

THERE ARE MANY WAYS OF SERVING COUSCOUS, EITHER AS AN ACCOMPANIMENT OR AS A DISH IN ITS OWN RIGHT AS IN THIS RECIPE. THIS DELICATE SALAD HAS A NORTH AFRICAN FLAVOUR THAT IS EXCELLENT WITH GRILLED CHICKEN OR KEBABS, OR MAKES A SUPERB PACKED LUNCH.

SERVES FOUR

INGREDIENTS
275g/10oz/1²/₃ cups couscous
550ml/18fl oz/2¹/₂ cups boiling
  vegetable stock
16–20 black olives
2 small courgettes (zucchini)
25g/1oz/¹/₄ cup flaked (sliced)
  almonds, toasted
60ml/4 tbsp olive oil
15ml/1 tbsp lemon juice
15ml/1 tbsp chopped fresh
  coriander (cilantro)
15ml/1 tbsp chopped fresh parsley
good pinch of ground cumin
good pinch of cayenne pepper
salt

1 Place the couscous in a bowl and pour over the boiling stock. Stir with a fork and then set aside for 10 minutes for the stock to be absorbed. Fluff up with a fork.

2 Halve the olives, discarding the stones (pits). Top and tail the courgettes and cut them into small julienne strips.

3 Carefully mix the courgettes, olives and toasted almonds into the couscous.

4 Mix together the olive oil, lemon juice, herbs, spices and a pinch of salt in a small bowl. Stir into the salad.

Energy 310kcal/1289kJ; Protein 5.7g; Carbohydrate 36g, of which sugars 0.6g; Fat 16.7g, of which saturates 2.1g; Cholesterol 0mg; Calcium 61mg; Fibre 1.5g; Sodium 286mg.

THAI-STYLE SEITAN SALAD

SEITAN IS MADE FROM WHEAT GLUTEN AND IS USUALLY USED AS A MEAT REPLACEMENT. LIKE TOFU, IT HAS A MILD FLAVOUR THAT BENEFITS FROM BEING MARINATED BEFORE COOKING.

3 Add the seitan and leave to marinate for at least 1 hour.

4 Remove the seitan from the marinade using tongs. Discard the marinade. Heat a wok until hot. Pour in the remaining olive oil and stir-fry the seitan for a few minutes until beginning to turn crisp.

5 Arrange the spinach, rocket leaves and tomatoes on a serving platter, then add the seitan. Spoon the dressing over and garnish with the chilli, coriander and basil.

SERVES FOUR

INGREDIENTS
    30ml/2 tbsp light soy sauce
    15ml/1 tbsp runny honey
    30ml/2 tbsp olive oil
    250g/9oz seitan, cut into
       2cm/³⁄₄in strips
    2 handfuls baby spinach leaves, tough
       stalks removed and leaves shredded
    2 handfuls rocket (arugula) leaves
    12 cherry tomatoes, halved
    1 fresh red chilli, seeded and cut
       into fine strips
    30ml/2 tbsp chopped fresh coriander
       (cilantro)
    1 handful fresh basil, leaves torn
For the dressing:
    45ml/3 tbsp lime juice
    30ml/2 tbsp olive oil
    10ml/2 tsp sesame oil
    15ml/1 tbsp light soy sauce
    15ml/1 tbsp grated fresh root ginger
    1 small garlic clove, finely chopped
    1 green chilli, seeded and
       finely chopped
    2.5ml/¹⁄₂ tsp palm sugar or soft light
       brown sugar

1 Mix together the ingredients for the dressing and set aside until step 5.

2 Mix together the soy sauce, honey and half the oil in a shallow dish.

COOK'S TIP
Use the sweetest cherry tomatoes you can find for this salad. Those ripened on the vine are often the best option.

VARIATION
Meat eaters will find that turkey makes a good alternative to seitan. Cut breast meat into strips and prepare as above, stir-frying until golden rather than crisp.

Energy 132kcal/547kJ; Protein 7g; Carbohydrate 3g, of which sugars 2.7g; Fat 10.3g, of which saturates 1.4g; Cholesterol 0mg; Calcium 431mg; Fibre 1.9g; Sodium 79mg.

FRUITY BROWN RICE SALAD

THE BROWN RICE GIVES THIS SALAD A PLEASANT NUTTY FLAVOUR AND TEXTURE THAT SUITS THE
ORIENTAL-STYLE DRESSING, WHILE THE PINEAPPLE PIECES ADD SWEETNESS AND A DISTINCT FLAVOUR.

SERVES FOUR TO SIX

INGREDIENTS

  115g/4oz/²⁄₃ cup brown rice
  1 small red (bell) pepper, seeded
    and diced
  200g/7oz can corn drained
  45ml/3 tbsp sultanas (golden raisins)
  225g/8oz can pineapple pieces
    in fruit juice
  15ml/1 tbsp light soy sauce
  15ml/1 tbsp sunflower oil
  15ml/1 tbsp hazelnut oil
  1 garlic clove, crushed
  5ml/1 tsp finely chopped fresh
    root ginger
  salt and ground black pepper
  4 spring onions (scallions), sliced,
    to garnish

1 Cook the brown rice in a large pan
of lightly salted boiling water for about
30 minutes, or until it is tender. Drain
thoroughly and cool. Meanwhile,
prepare the garnish. Slice the spring
onions at an angle, as shown,
then set aside.

2 Tip the rice into a large serving bowl
and add the red pepper, corn and
sultanas. Drain the pineapple pieces,
reserving the juice, then add them to
the rice mixture and toss lightly.

COOK'S TIP
Hazelnut oil gives a distinctive flavour to
any salad dressing. Like olive oil, it
contains mainly mono-unsaturated fats.

3 Pour the reserved pineapple juice
into a clean screw-top jar. Add the soy
sauce, sunflower and hazelnut oils,
garlic and root ginger. Season with salt
and pepper. Close the jar tightly and
shake well to combine.

4 Pour the dressing over the salad and
toss well. Scatter the spring onions over
the top and serve.

Energy 191kcal/806kJ; Protein 2.9g; Carbohydrate 36.3g, of which sugars 15.2g; Fat 4.8g, of which saturates 0.7g; Cholesterol 0mg; Calcium 14mg; Fibre 1.6g; Sodium 272mg.

GOAT'S CHEESE, FIG ᴬᴺᴰ COUSCOUS SALAD

FRESH FIGS AND WALNUTS ARE PERFECT PARTNERS FOR COUSCOUS AND TOASTED BUCKWHEAT. THE OLIVE AND NUT OIL DRESSING CONTAINS NO VINEGAR, DEPENDING INSTEAD ON THE ACIDITY OF THE GOAT'S CHEESE. THIS SALAD IS SUBSTANTIAL ENOUGH TO MAKE A COMPLETE MEAL.

SERVES FOUR

INGREDIENTS
175g/6oz/1 cup couscous
30ml/2 tbsp toasted buckwheat
1 egg, hard-boiled
30ml/2 tbsp chopped fresh parsley
60ml/4 tbsp olive oil
45ml/3 tbsp walnut oil
115g/4oz rocket (arugula) leaves
½ frisée lettuce
175g/6oz crumbly white
  goat's cheese
50g/2oz/½ cup broken
  walnuts, toasted
4 ripe figs, trimmed and almost cut
  into four (leave the pieces joined at
  the base)

1 Place the couscous and toasted buckwheat in a bowl, cover with boiling water and leave to soak for 15 minutes. Place in a sieve to drain off any remaining water, then spread out on a metal tray and allow to cool.

2 Shell the hard-boiled egg and grate finely.

3 Toss the grated egg, parsley, couscous and buckwheat together in a bowl. Combine the olive and walnut oils and use half to moisten the couscous mixture.

4 Toss the salad leaves in the remaining oil and distribute among four large serving plates.

5 Pile couscous mixture in the centre of each plate and crumble the goat's cheese over the top. Scatter with toasted walnuts, place a fig in the centre of each plate and serve.

Energy 599kcal/2488kJ; Protein 17.3g; Carbohydrate 40.9g, of which sugars 12.6g; Fat 41.7g, of which saturates 11.3g; Cholesterol 88mg; Calcium 173mg; Fibre 2.9g; Sodium 299mg.

EGG AND FENNEL TABBOULEH WITH NUTS

TABBOULEH IS A WELL-KNOWN AND POPULAR MIDDLE EASTERN SALAD OF BULGUR WHEAT, FLAVOURED WITH LOTS OF PARSLEY, MINT, LEMON JUICE AND GARLIC. THIS VARIATION INCLUDES DELICATE EGG AND FENNEL, SWEET, CRISP SPRING ONIONS AND THE CRUNCH OF TOASTED HAZLENUTS — DELICIOUS.

SERVES FOUR

INGREDIENTS

- 250g/9oz/1¼ cups bulgur wheat
- 4 small eggs
- 1 fennel bulb
- 1 bunch of spring onions (scallions), chopped
- 25g/1oz/½ cup drained sun-dried tomatoes in oil, sliced
- 45ml/3 tbsp chopped fresh parsley
- 30ml/2 tbsp chopped fresh mint
- 75g/3oz/½ cup black olives
- 60ml/4 tbsp olive oil
- 30ml/2 tbsp garlic oil
- 30ml/2 tbsp lemon juice
- 50g/2oz/½ cup chopped hazelnuts, toasted
- pitta bread, warmed, to serve
- salt and ground black pepper

1 Place the bulgur wheat in a bowl; pour in boiling water to cover and leave to soak for about 15 minutes.

2 Drain the bulgur wheat in a metal sieve, and place the sieve over a pan of boiling water. Cover the pan and sieve with a lid and steam for about 10 minutes. Fluff up the grains with a fork and spread out on a metal tray. Set aside to cool.

3 Hard-boil the eggs for 8 minutes. Cool under running water, peel and quarter, or, using an egg slicer, slice not quite all the way through.

4 Halve and finely slice the fennel. Boil in salted water for 6 minutes, drain and cool under running water.

5 Combine the eggs, fennel, spring onions, sun-dried tomatoes, parsley, mint and olives with the bulgur wheat. Dress with olive oil, garlic oil and lemon juice and sprinkle with hazelnuts. Season well and serve with pitta bread.

COOK'S TIP

If you are short of time, soak the bulgur wheat in boiling water for about 20 minutes until the grains are tender. Drain and rinse under cold water to cool, then drain thoroughly.

Energy 512kcal/2129kJ; Protein 15.7g; Carbohydrate 50.9g, of which sugars 2.8g; Fat 28g, of which saturates 4.1g; Cholesterol 190mg; Calcium 135mg; Fibre 3.9g; Sodium 509mg.

MUSHROOM PILAU

THIS DISH IS SIMPLICITY ITSELF: THE BASMATI RICE IS INFUSED WITH A DELICIOUS BLEND OF SPICES. SERVE WITH ANY INDIAN DISH OR WITH ROAST LAMB OR CHICKEN.

2 Add the ghee or butter. When it has melted, add the mushrooms and fry for 2–3 minutes more.

3 Add the rice, ginger and garam masala. Stir-fry over a low heat for 2–3 minutes, then stir in the water and a little salt. Bring to the boil, then cover tightly and simmer over a very low heat for 10 minutes.

SERVES FOUR

INGREDIENTS
- 30ml/2 tbsp vegetable oil
- 2 shallots, finely chopped
- 1 garlic clove, crushed
- 3 green cardamom pods
- 25g/1oz/2 tbsp ghee or butter
- 175g/6oz/2½ cups button mushrooms, sliced
- 225g/8oz/generous 1 cup basmati rice, soaked
- 5ml/1 tsp grated fresh root ginger
- good pinch of garam masala
- 450ml/¾ pint/scant 2 cups water
- 15ml/1 tbsp chopped fresh coriander (cilantro)
- salt

1 Heat the oil in a pan and fry the shallots, garlic and cardamom pods over a medium heat for 3–4 minutes.

4 Remove the casserole from the heat. Leave to stand, covered, for 5 minutes. Add the chopped coriander and fork it through the rice. Spoon into a serving bowl and serve at once.

Energy 309kcal/1286kJ; Protein 5.2g; Carbohydrate 46.3g, of which sugars 1g; Fat 11.2g, of which saturates 4g; Cholesterol 13mg; Calcium 18mg; Fibre 0.7g; Sodium 41mg.

GARLIC CHIVE RICE WITH MUSHROOMS

A WIDE RANGE OF MUSHROOMS IS READILY AVAILABLE. THEY COMBINE WELL WITH RICE AND GARLIC CHIVES TO MAKE A TASTY ACCOMPANIMENT TO VEGETARIAN DISHES, FISH OR CHICKEN.

SERVES FOUR

INGREDIENTS
  350g/12oz/generous 1¾ cups
    long grain rice
  60ml/4 tbsp groundnut (peanut) oil
  1 small onion, finely chopped
  2 green chillies, seeded and
    finely chopped
  25g/1oz garlic chives, chopped
  15g/½oz fresh coriander (cilantro)
  600ml/1 pint/2½ cups vegetable or
    mushroom stock
  2.5ml/½ tsp sea salt
  250g/9oz mixed mushrooms,
    thickly sliced
  50g/2oz cashew nuts, fried in 15ml/
    1 tbsp olive oil until golden brown
  ground black pepper

1 Wash and drain the rice. Heat half the oil in a pan and cook the onion and chillies over a gentle heat, stirring occasionally, for 10–12 minutes until soft.

2 Set half the garlic chives aside. Cut the stalks off the coriander and set the leaves aside. Purée the remaining chives and the coriander stalks with the stock in a food processor or blender.

3 Add the rice to the onions and fry over a low heat, stirring frequently, for 4–5 minutes. Pour in the stock mixture, then stir in the salt and a good grinding of black pepper. Bring to the boil, then stir and reduce the heat to very low. Cover tightly with a lid and cook for 15–20 minutes, or until the rice has absorbed all the liquid.

4 Remove the pan from the heat and lay a clean, folded dishtowel over the pan, under the lid, and press on the lid to wedge it firmly in place. Leave the rice to stand for a further 10 minutes, allowing the towel to absorb the steam while the rice becomes completely tender.

VARIATION
For a higher-fibre alternative make this dish with brown rice. Increase the cooking time in step 3 to 25–30 minutes or follow the packet instructions.

5 Meanwhile, heat the remaining oil in a frying pan and cook the mushrooms for 5–6 minutes until tender and browned. Add the remaining garlic chives and cook for another 1–2 minutes.

6 Stir the cooked mushroom and chive mixture and chopped coriander leaves into the rice. Adjust the seasoning to taste, then transfer to a warmed serving dish and serve immediately, scattered with the fried cashew nuts.

Energy 504kcal/2100kJ; Protein 10.4g; Carbohydrate 73.8g, of which sugars 1.8g; Fat 18.2g, of which saturates 2.6g; Cholesterol 0mg; Calcium 41mg; Fibre 1.6g; Sodium 533mg.

COUSCOUS WITH DRIED FRUIT AND NUTS

THIS DISH OF STEAMED COUSCOUS WITH DRIED FRUIT AND NUTS, TOPPED WITH SUGAR AND CINNAMON, IS DELICIOUS SERVED WITH SPICY TAGINES OR GRILLED OR ROASTED MEAT AND POULTRY DISHES. TRY IT AS A SIDE DISH AT YOUR NEXT BARBECUE.

SERVES SIX

INGREDIENTS
  500g/1¼lb medium couscous
  600ml/1 pint/2½ cups warm water
  5ml/1 tsp salt
  pinch of saffron threads
  45ml/3 tbsp sunflower oil
  30ml/2 tbsp olive oil
  a little butter
  115g/4oz/½ cup dried apricots, cut
    into slivers
  75g/3oz/½ cup dried dates, chopped
  75g/3oz/generous ½ cup raisins
  115g/4oz/1 cup blanched almonds,
    cut into slivers
  75g/3oz/¾ cup pistachio nuts
  10ml/2 tsp ground cinnamon
  45ml/3 tbsp sugar

1 Preheat the oven to 180°C/350°F/ Gas 4. Put the couscous in a bowl. Mix the water, salt and saffron and pour it over the couscous, stirring. Leave to stand for 10 minutes, or until the grains are plump and tender. Add the sunflower oil and, using your fingers, rub it through the grains.

2 In a heavy pan, heat the olive oil and butter and stir in the apricots, dates, raisins, most of the almonds (reserve some for garnish) and pistachio nuts. Cook until the raisins plump up, then tip the nuts and fruit into the couscous and toss together.

3 Tip the couscous into an ovenproof dish and cover with foil. Place in the oven for about 20 minutes, until heated through.

4 Toast the reserved slivered almonds. Pile the hot couscous in a mound on a large serving dish and sprinkle with the cinnamon and sugar – these are usually sprinkled in stripes down the mound. Scatter the toasted almonds over the top and serve hot.

Energy 592kcal/2471kJ; Protein 12.5g; Carbohydrate 77.1g, of which sugars 33.5g; Fat 27.8g, of which saturates 3g; Cholesterol 0mg; Calcium 105mg; Fibre 4.1g; Sodium 81mg.

VEGETABLE COUSCOUS WITH HARISSA

THIS SPICY DISH MAKES AN EXCELLENT VEGETARIAN MAIN COURSE, OR CAN BE SERVED AS AN ACCOMPANIMENT. COUSCOUS IS ONE OF THE EASIEST GRAINS TO PREPARE AND ONLY TAKES A MATTER OF MINUTES. SINCE IT HAS A RELATIVELY MILD FLAVOUR IT GOES WELL WITH AROMATIC SPICES.

SERVES FOUR

INGREDIENTS

45ml/3 tbsp olive oil
1 onion, chopped
2 garlic cloves, crushed
5ml/1 tsp ground cumin
5ml/1 tsp paprika
400g/14oz can chopped tomatoes
300ml/½ pint/1¼ cups
  vegetable stock
1 cinnamon stick
generous pinch of saffron threads
4 baby aubergines (eggplants),
  quartered
8 baby courgettes (zucchini),
  trimmed
8 baby carrots
225g/8oz/1⅓ cups couscous
425g/15oz can chickpeas, drained
175g/6oz/¾ cup pitted prunes
45ml/3 tbsp chopped fresh parsley
45ml/3 tbsp chopped fresh
  coriander (cilantro)
10–15ml/2–3 tsp harissa
salt

1 Heat the olive oil in a large pan. Add the onion and garlic and cook gently for 5 minutes until soft. Add the cumin and paprika and cook, stirring, for 1 minute.

2 Add the tomatoes, stock, cinnamon stick, saffron, aubergines, courgettes and carrots, and season with salt. Bring to the boil, cover, lower the heat and cook gently for 20 minutes until the vegetables are just tender.

3 Line a steamer or colander with a double thickness of muslin (cheesecloth). Soak the couscous according to the instructions on the packet.

COOK'S TIP
Harissa is a chilli-hot, spicy paste from North Africa. You can buy it ready made from selected supermarkets and specialist shops.

4 Add the chickpeas and prunes to the vegetables, stir and cook for 5 minutes.

5 Spread the couscous in the prepared steamer. place the steamer on top of the vegetables, cover and cook for 5 minutes until the couscous is hot.

6 Stir the herbs into the vegetables. Heap the couscous on to a serving dish. Using a slotted spoon, remove the vegetables from the pan and add to the couscous. Spoon over a little sauce and toss gently. Stir the harissa into the remaining sauce and serve separately.

Energy 452kcal/1897kJ; Protein 14.8g; Carbohydrate 72.9g, of which sugars 27.4g; Fat 13.1g, of which saturates 1.8g; Cholesterol 0mg; Calcium 143mg; Fibre 12.2g; Sodium 259mg.

BASMATI RICE AND NUT PILAFF

VEGETARIANS WILL LOVE THIS SIMPLE PILAFF. ADD WILD OR CULTIVATED MUSHROOMS AND DICED CARROTS OR COURGETTES TO MAKE THE DISH MORE SUBSTANTIAL, IF YOU LIKE.

SERVES FOUR

INGREDIENTS

15–30ml/1–2 tbsp sunflower oil
1 onion, chopped
1 garlic clove, crushed
1 large carrot, coarsely grated
225g/8oz/generous 1 cup basmati
  rice, soaked
5ml/1 tsp cumin seeds
10ml/2 tsp ground coriander
10ml/2 tsp black mustard seeds
  (optional)
4 green cardamom pods
450ml/¾ pint/scant 2 cups vegetable
  stock or water
1 bay leaf
75g/3oz/½ cup shelled walnuts and/or
  unsalted cashew nuts
salt and ground black pepper
fresh parsley or coriander (cilantro)
  sprigs, to garnish

1 Heat the oil in a large frying pan. Add the onion, garlic and carrot and cook for 3–4 minutes, stirring occasionally.

2 Drain the rice and add it to the pan with the cumin seeds, ground coriander, black mustard seeds and the green cardamom pods. Cook for 1 minute, stirring to coat the grains in oil.

COOK'S TIP
Basmati rice has an aromatic nut-like flavour that goes well with curries and pilaffs.

3 Pour in the vegetable stock or water, add the bay leaf and season well with salt and pepper. Bring to the boil, then lower the heat, cover and simmer very gently for 10–12 minutes.

4 Remove the frying pan from the heat without lifting the lid. Leave to stand in a warm place for about 5 minutes, then check the rice. If it is cooked, there will be small steam holes on the surface of the rice. Remove the bay leaf and the cardamom pods.

5 Stir the walnuts and/or cashew nuts into the rice mixture. Taste to check the seasoning and add more salt and pepper if necessary. Spoon into warmed individual bowls or on to a large platter, garnish with the sprigs of fresh parsley or coriander and serve immediately.

COOK'S TIP
Use whichever nuts you prefer in this pilaff – even unsalted peanuts taste good – although almonds, brazil nuts, cashew nuts or pistachio nuts add a slightly more exotic flavour.

Energy 370kcal/1538kJ; Protein 7.3g; Carbohydrate 48.7g, of which sugars 3.2g; Fat 16g, of which saturates 1.4g; Cholesterol 0mg; Calcium 38mg; Fibre 1.5g; Sodium 8mg.

JAMAICAN RICE AND PEAS

IN JAMAICA THIS HAS BECOME ALMOST A NATIONAL DISH. THE "PEAS" ARE ACTUALLY RED KIDNEY BEANS WHICH GIVE COLOUR AND SUBSTANCE TO THE COCONUT RICE.

SERVES FOUR TO SIX

INGREDIENTS

150g/5oz dried red kidney beans
500ml/17fl oz/2¼ cups water
1 tsp salt
15ml/1 tbsp vegetable oil
15ml/1 large onion, chopped
3 garlic cloves, chopped
2 fresh red chillies, seeded and chopped
5ml/1 tsp dried thyme
300g/11oz long grain rice
400g/14oz can coconut milk

1 Soak the kidney beans overnight in plenty of cold water. Drain and rinse, then put them into a pan. Cover with fresh cold water and bring to the boil. Allow to boil vigorously for 10 minutes, then reduce the heat, cover the pan, and simmer for 1 hour or until tender.

2 Drain the beans then return them to the pan and cover with 300ml/½ pint/1¼ cups of the water and add the salt. Bring to the boil, then reduce the heat and simmer, covered, for 15 minutes.

3 Meanwhile, heat the oil in a large pan and fry the onion for 10 minutes until softened. Add the garlic, chillies and thyme. Fry, stirring, for 1 minute, then add the rice. Stir well until the rice is coated in the onion mixture.

4 Pour in the coconut milk, the remaining water and the beans and their cooking water. Bring up to the boil, then reduce the heat, stir well and cover the pan. Simmer over a low heat for 25–30 minutes until the rice is tender and the liquid has been absorbed. Remove from the heat and allow the rice and beans to stand for 5 minutes in the covered pan before transferring to a warmed dish.

Energy 295kcal/1240kJ; Protein 10g; Carbohydrate 58.2g, of which sugars 6.7g; Fat 2.7g, of which saturates 0.4g; Cholesterol 0mg; Calcium 66mg; Fibre 4.6g; Sodium 79mg.

BUCKWHEAT KASHA

KASHA IS A TYPE OF RUSSIAN PORRIDGE, MADE FROM A VARIETY OF GRAINS INCLUDING WHEAT, BARLEY, MILLET AND OATS. THE MOST POPULAR IS BUCKWHEAT, WHICH HAS A DISTINCTIVE NUTTY FLAVOUR THAT BENEFITS FROM TOASTING BEFORE USE.

SERVES FOUR

INGREDIENTS
175g/6oz/scant 1 cup buckwheat
740ml/1¼ pints/3 cups boiling stock
25g/1oz/2 tbsp butter
pinch of freshly grated nutmeg
115g/4oz rindless smoked streaky
 (fatty) bacon, chopped
salt and ground black pepper

1 Dry-fry the buckwheat in a non-stick frying pan for 2 minutes, or until very lightly toasted. Transfer the buckwheat to a pan and add the stock.

COOK'S TIP
It is possible to buy toasted buckwheat. In this case, simply put the buckwheat in a pan and add the stock.

2 Simmer for 15–20 minutes, stirring occasionally to prevent it from sticking. When almost dry, remove from the heat.

3 Add the butter to the buckwheat, season and add the nutmeg. Cover with a lid and let stand for 5 minutes. Meanwhile, dry-fry the bacon for 5 minutes, until lightly browned and crispy. Sprinkle over the kasha. Serve.

Energy 280kcal/1166kJ; Protein 8.8g; Carbohydrate 33.4g, of which sugars 0g; Fat 12.7g, of which saturates 5.6g; Cholesterol 32mg; Calcium 22mg; Fibre 4.4g; Sodium 402mg.

CARTERS' MILLET

THIS DISH ORIGINATED IN SOUTHERN UKRAINE, WHERE IT WAS ONCE COOKED OVER OPEN FIRES. IT IS IDEAL SERVED WITH MEAT, POULTRY OR VEGETABLES.

SERVES FOUR

INGREDIENTS
225g/8oz/scant 1½ cups millet
600ml/1 pint/2½ cups
 vegetable stock
115g/4oz lardons or rindless smoked
 streaky (fatty) bacon, chopped
15ml/1 tbsp olive oil
1 small onion, thinly sliced
225g/8oz/3 cups small field
 mushrooms, sliced
15ml/1 tbsp chopped fresh mint
salt and ground black pepper

1 Rinse the millet in a sieve under cold running water. Put in a pan with the stock, bring to the boil and simmer, until the stock has been absorbed.

2 Dry-fry the lardons or bacon in a non-stick pan for 5 minutes, until brown and crisp. Remove and set aside.

3 Add the oil to the pan and cook the onion and mushrooms for 10 minutes, until beginning to brown.

4 Add the bacon, and the onion and mushroom mixture to the millet. Stir in the mint and season. Heat gently for 1–2 minutes before serving.

Energy 316kcal/1317kJ; Protein 9g; Carbohydrate 43.8g, of which sugars 1g; Fat 10.8g, of which saturates 2.8g; Cholesterol 19mg; Calcium 31mg; Fibre 0.8g; Sodium 377mg.

COUSCOUS-STUFFED SWEET PEPPERS

COUSCOUS-STUFFED SWEET PEPPERSTHESE BELL PEPPERS ARE SOFTENED IN BOILING WATER TO ENSURE REALLY TENDER RESULTS. CHOOSE RED, ORANGE OR YELLOW PEPPERS FOR THE SWEETEST FLAVOUR.

SERVES FOUR

INGREDIENTS

4 (bell) peppers
75g/3oz//½ cup instant couscous
75ml/2½fl oz/⅓ cup boiling
    vegetable stock
15ml/1 tbsp olive oil
10ml/2 tsp white wine vinegar
50g/2oz dried apricots, finely
    chopped
75g/3oz feta cheese, cut into tiny
    cubes
3 ripe tomatoes, skinned, seeded
    and chopped
45ml/3 tbsp toasted pine nuts
30ml/2 tbsp chopped fresh parsley
salt and ground black pepper
flat leaf parsely, to garnish

1 Halve the peppers lengthways, then remove the core and seeds. Place the peppers in a large heatproof bowl and pour over boiling water to cover. Leave to stand for about 3 minutes, then drain thoroughly and set aside.

2 Meanwhile, put the couscous in a small bowl and pour over the stock. Leave to stand for about 5 minutes until all the stock has been absorbed.

3 Using a fork, fluff up the couscous, then stir in the oil, vinegar, apricots, feta cheese, tomatoes, pine nuts and parsley, and season to taste with salt and ground black pepper.

4 Preheat the oven to 190°C/375°F/ Gas 5.

5 Fill the peppers with couscous mixture, gently packing it down using the back of a spoon.

6 Place the peppers filling side up in a lightly greased ovenproof dish, and bake for 20–25 minutes until golden.

VARIATION
Instead of feta cheese, you could grate any hard cheese on to the surface of the stuffed peppers.

Energy 303kcal/1266kJ; Protein 33.7g; Carbohydrate 33.6g, of which sugars 17g; Fat 15.8g, of which saturates 3.9g; Cholesterol 113mg; Calcium 105mg; Fibre 4.3g; Sodium 285mg.

OATMEAL SKIRLIE

OATMEAL IS USED TO MAKE SKIRLIE, A SIMPLE PREPARATION THAT CAN BE USED FOR STUFFINGS AND IS GOOD WITH ROAST MEATS. IT IS TRADITIONALLY COOKED IN LARD BUT MANY PEOPLE PREFER BUTTER.

SERVES FOUR

INGREDIENTS
  50g/2oz/¼ cup butter
  1 onion, finely chopped
  175g/6oz/scant 2 cups medium
    oatmeal
  salt and ground black pepper

VARIATION
To add a lovely rich flavour to the skirlie, grate in a little nutmeg and add a pinch of cinnamon towards the end.

1 Melt the butter in a pan over a medium heat and add the onion. Fry gently until it is softened and very slightly browned.

2 Stir in the oatmeal and season with salt and ground black pepper. Cook gently for 10 minutes. Taste for seasoning and serve immediately.

Energy 282kcal/1182kJ; Protein 6g; Carbohydrate 34.9g, of which sugars 2.2g; Fat 14.2g, of which saturates 6.5g; Cholesterol 27mg; Calcium 36mg; Fibre 3.5g; Sodium 91mg.

VEGETARIAN

Grains are essential in many vegetarian dishes, where they frequently provide the carbohydrate content and texture. Rice, wheat and other cereals are the basis for a wide variety of classic dishes including Layered Polenta Bake, Buckwheat with Pasta, and Barley Risotto with Roasted Squash. These dishes are highly versatile and a delight to prepare, being healthy, colourful and full of flavour.

WILD RICE PILAFF

WILD RICE ISN'T ACTUALLY RICE, BUT IS A TYPE OF WILD GRASS. CALL IT WHAT YOU WILL, IT HAS A WONDERFUL NUTTY FLAVOUR AND COMBINES WELL WITH LONG GRAIN RICE IN THIS FRUITY MIXTURE. TOP WITH SLICES OF HALLOUMI CHEESE FOR A MORE SUBSTANTIAL VEGETARIAN DISH.

SERVES SIX

INGREDIENTS
    200g/7oz/1 cup wild rice
    40g/1½oz/3 tbsp butter
    ½ onion, finely chopped
    200g/7oz/1 cup long grain rice
    475ml/16fl oz/2 cups vegetable stock
    75g/3oz/¾ cup slivered or
        flaked (sliced) almonds
    115g/4oz/⅔ cup sultanas (golden
        raisins)
    30ml/2 tbsp chopped fresh parsley
    salt and ground black pepper

1 Bring a large pan of water to the boil. Add the wild rice and 5ml/1 tsp salt. Lower the heat, cover and simmer gently for 45–60 minutes, until the rice is tender. Drain well.

2 Meanwhile, melt 15g/½oz/1 tbsp of the butter in another pan. Add the onion and cook over a medium heat for about 5 minutes until it is just softened. Stir in the long grain rice and cook for 1 minute more.

3 Stir in the stock and bring to the boil. Cover and simmer gently for 30–40 minutes, until the rice is tender and the liquid has been absorbed.

4 Melt the remaining butter in a small pan. Add the almonds and cook until they are just golden. Set aside.

5 Put the rice mixture in a bowl and add the almonds, sultanas and half the parsley. Stir to mix. Taste and adjust the seasoning if necessary. Transfer to a warmed serving dish, sprinkle with the remaining parsley and serve.

COOK'S TIP
This dish must be made with well-flavoured stock. If you haven't time to make your own, use a carton or can of good quality stock.

Energy 424kcal/1769kJ; Protein 8.4g; Carbohydrate 68.3g, of which sugars 14.6g; Fat 13g, of which saturates 4g; Cholesterol 14mg; Calcium 69mg; Fibre 1.7g; Sodium 48mg.

BULGUR WHEAT AND ASPARAGUS PILAFF

NUTTY-TEXTURED BULGUR WHEAT IS USUALLY SIMPLY SOAKED IN BOILING WATER UNTIL IT IS SOFTENED, BUT IT CAN BE COOKED LIKE RICE TO MAKE A PILAFF. HERE IT IS COMBINED WITH BROAD BEANS, HERBS, AND LEMON AND ORANGE RINDS, WHICH ADD A FRESH, SPRINGTIME FLAVOUR.

SERVES FOUR

INGREDIENTS
250g/9oz/1½ cups bulgur wheat
750–900ml/1¼–1½ pints/3–3¾
   cups warm vegetable stock
225g/8oz asparagus spears
225g/8oz/2 cups frozen broad (fava)
   beans, thawed
8 spring onions (scallions), chopped
15ml/1 tbsp grated lemon rind
15ml/1 tbsp grated orange rind
40g/1½oz/3 tbsp butter, cut into
   small pieces
60ml/4 tbsp chopped fresh flat
   leaf parsley
30ml/2 tbsp chopped fresh dill, plus
   extra sprigs to garnish
salt and ground black pepper

1 Place the bulgur wheat in a shallow, ovenproof earthenware dish and pour over 600ml/1 pint/2½ cups of the stock. Season with salt and pepper.

VARIATIONS
• Use fresh green beans and either fresh or frozen peas in place of the asparagus and broad beans and, instead of using dill, stir in plenty of chopped fresh mint along with the parsley.
• If you'd like to add a little extra colour to the pilaff, then stir in some finely shredded red (bell) pepper, or some peeled and seeded wedges of tomato.

2 Cut the asparagus spears into 2.5cm/1in lengths, discarding any hard, woody ends from the stems. Add the asparagus pieces to the dish and gently stir these into the bulgur wheat.

3 Cover the dish tightly and place in an unheated oven. Set the oven to 200°C/400°F/Gas 6 and then cook the bulgur wheat and asparagus for 20 minutes.

4 Meanwhile pop the broad beans out of their skins and stir them into the bulgur pilaff, adding a little more stock at the same time. Re-cover the dish and return it to the oven for about 10 minutes.

5 Stir in the spring onions, grated lemon and orange rind. Add a little more stock, if necessary. Cover and return to the oven for 5 minutes.

6 Dot the pieces of butter over the top of the pilaff and leave to stand, covered, for 5 minutes.

7 Add the parsley and dill to the pilaff and stir with a fork. Add salt and plenty of black pepper. Serve hot, garnished with sprigs of fresh dill.

COOK'S TIP
Leaving the bulgur wheat to stand for 5 minutes after cooking helps to give it a light, fluffy texture.

Energy 368kcal/1536kJ; Protein 13.4g; Carbohydrate 56.7g, of which sugars 3g; Fat 10.4g, of which saturates 5.4g; Cholesterol 21mg; Calcium 134mg; Fibre 6.2g; Sodium 79mg.

FRESH HERB RISOTTO

DISTINCTIVE, NUTTY-FLAVOURED WILD RICE IS COMBINED WITH ARBORIO RICE TO CREATE THIS CREAMY, COMFORTING RISOTTO. SPRINKLE WITH FRESHLY GRATED PARMESAN BEFORE SERVING.

3 Pour in the wine and bring to the boil. Reduce the heat and cook for 10 minutes until the wine has evaporated. Add the stock, a little at a time, and simmer, stirring, for 20–25 minutes until the liquid is absorbed and the rice is creamy. Season well.

4 Add the herbs and wild rice; heat for 2 minutes, stirring frequently. Stir in two-thirds of the Parmesan and cook until melted. Serve sprinkled with the remaining Parmesan.

SERVES FOUR

INGREDIENTS
90g/3½oz/½ cup wild rice
15ml/1 tbsp butter
15ml/1 tbsp olive oil
1 small onion, finely chopped
450g/1lb/2½ cups arborio rice
300ml/½ pint/1¼ cups dry white wine
1.2 litres/2 pints/5 cups vegetable stock
45ml/3 tbsp chopped fresh oregano
45ml/3 tbsp chopped fresh chives
60ml/4 tbsp chopped fresh flat leaf parsley
60ml/4 tbsp chopped fresh basil
75g/3oz/1 cup freshly grated Parmesan cheese
salt and ground black pepper

1 Cook the wild rice in boiling salted water according to the instructions on the packet. Drain and set aside.

2 Heat the butter and oil in a large heavy pan. When the butter has melted, add the onion and cook for 3 minutes, Add the arborio rice and cook for 2 minutes, stirring to coat it in the oil mixture.

COOK'S TIP
Risotto rice is essential to achieve the right creamy texture in this dish. Other types of rice simply will not do. Fresh herbs are also a must, but you can use tarragon, chervil, marjoram or thyme instead of those listed here.

BUCKWHEAT WITH PASTA

THIS COMBINATION OF BUCKWHEAT, MUSHROOMS AND BOW-SHAPED PASTA IS A CLASSIC DISH CALLED KASHA. TO PEOPLE WHO ARE NEW TO BUCKWHEAT IT MAY TASTE GRAINY.

SERVES FOUR TO SIX

INGREDIENTS

25g/1oz dried well-flavoured
  mushrooms, such as ceps
500ml/17fl oz/2¼ cups boiling
  stock or water
45ml/3 tbsp vegetable oil or
  40g/1½oz/3 tbsp butter
3–4 onions, thinly sliced
250g/9oz mushrooms, sliced
300g/11oz/1½ cups whole, coarse,
  medium or fine buckwheat
200g/7oz pasta bows
salt and ground black pepper

3 In a large, heavy frying pan, toast the buckwheat over a high heat for 2–3 minutes, stirring. Reduce the heat.

4 Stir the remaining boiling stock or water and the reserved mushroom soaking liquid into the buckwheat, cover the pan, and cook for about 10 minutes until the buckwheat is just tender and the liquid has been absorbed.

5 Meanwhile, cook the pasta in a large pan of salted boiling water as directed on the packet, or until just tender, then drain.

6 When the kasha is cooked, toss in the onions and mushrooms, and the pasta. Season and serve hot.

1 Put the dried mushrooms in a bowl, pour over half the boiling stock or water and leave to stand for 20–30 minutes, until reconstituted. Remove the mushrooms from the liquid, then strain and reserve the liquid.

2 Heat the oil or butter in a frying pan, add the onions and fry for 5–10 minutes until softened and beginning to brown. Remove the onions to a plate, then add the sliced mushrooms to the pan and fry briefly. Add the soaked mushrooms and cook for 2–3 minutes. Return the onions to the pan and set aside.

VARIATION
To cook kasha without mushrooms, omit both kinds and simply add all of the boiling stock in step 4.

Energy 364kcal/1529kJ; Protein 10.3g; Carbohydrate 67g, of which sugars 4g; Fat 7.3g, of which saturates 3.6g; Cholesterol 14mg; Calcium 47mg; Fibre 2.2g; Sodium 48mg.

SAVOY CABBAGE WITH MUSHROOM BARLEY

THE FIRM TEXTURE OF SAVOY CABBAGE MAKES A GOOD CONTAINER FOR AN EARTHY, RICH STUFFING OF BARLEY AND MIXED CULTIVATED AND WILD MUSHROOMS.

SERVES FOUR

INGREDIENTS

50g/2oz/4 tbsp unsalted (sweet)
  butter
2 onions, chopped
1 celery stick, sliced
225g/8oz assorted wild and
  cultivated mushrooms
175g/6oz/1¼ cups pearl barley
1 fresh thyme sprig
750ml/1¼ pints/3⅔ cups water
30ml/2 tbsp almond or cashew
  nut butter
½ vegetable stock cube
1 Savoy cabbage
salt and ground black pepper

1 Melt the butter in a large heavy pan, add the onions and celery and fry for 6–8 minutes until soft. Add the mushrooms and cook until they release their juices, then add the barley, thyme, water and the nut butter. Bring to the boil, cover and simmer for 30 minutes. Add the ½ stock cube and simmer for another 20 minutes. Season to taste.

2 Separate the cabbage leaves and cut away the thick stem. Blanch the leaves in salted boiling water for 3–4 minutes. Drain and refresh under cold running water. Drain again.

3 Place a 46cm/18in square of muslin (cheesecloth) over a steaming basket. Reconstruct the cabbage by lining the muslin with large cabbage leaves. Spread a layer of mushroom barley over the leaves.

4 Cover with a second layer of leaves and filling. Continue until the centre is full. Draw together opposite corners of the muslin and tie firmly. Place the cabbage in a steaming basket, set in a pan containing 2.5cm/1in of simmering water, Cover and steam for 30 minutes. To serve, place on a warmed serving plate, untie the muslin and carefully pull it away from underneath the cabbage.

COOK'S TIPS
• A range of nut butters is available in all leading health food stores.
• If planning ahead, the cabbage can be assembled well in advance before the final cooking.
• To ensure richness and flavour use a good portion of ceps, chicken of the woods and field mushrooms.

Energy 354kcal/1485kJ; Protein 8.7g; Carbohydrate 47.5g, of which sugars 9.6g; Fat 15.6g, of which saturates 7.5g; Cholesterol 27mg; Calcium 103mg; Fibre 4.7g; Sodium 127mg.

GOAT'S CHEESE WITH GRAINS AND WALNUTS

ROBUSTLY FLAVOURED BUCKWHEAT IS OFTEN COMBINED WITH OTHER GRAINS. COUSCOUS ALLOWS THE FLAVOUR OF BUCKWHEAT, GOAT'S CHEESE, DRIED CEPS AND TOASTED WALNUTS TO COME THROUGH.

SERVES FOUR

INGREDIENTS

175g/6oz/1 cup couscous
45ml/3 tbsp buckwheat
½oz/15g/¼ cup dried ceps or
 bay boletus
3 eggs
60ml/4 tbsp chopped fresh parsley
10ml/2 tsp chopped fresh thyme
60ml/4 tbsp olive oil
45ml/3 tbsp walnut oil
175g/6oz/1½ cups crumbly white
 goat's cheese
50g/2oz/½ cup broken walnuts,
 toasted
salt and ground black pepper
salad and rye bread, to serve

1 Place the couscous, buckwheat and ceps in a bowl, cover with boiling water and leave to soak for 15 minutes. Drain off any excess liquid.

2 Place the mixture in a large non-stick frying pan, add the eggs, season well, then scramble with a flat wooden spoon over a moderate heat.

3 Stir in the parsley, thyme, olive oil, walnut oil, goat's cheese and walnuts. Season to taste with salt and pepper.

4 Transfer to a large serving dish and serve hot with rye bread and salad.

Energy 597kcal/2475kJ; Protein 19.7g; Carbohydrate 32.2g, of which sugars 1g; Fat 44g, of which saturates 12g; Cholesterol 183mg; Calcium 127mg; Fibre 1g; Sodium 321mg.

GRILLED POLENTA

*SLICES OF GRILLED POLENTA ARE DELICIOUS TOPPED WITH SLOWLY CARAMELIZED ONIONS AND
BUBBLING TALEGGIO CHEESE. SERVE WITH RADICCHIO LEAVES.*

SERVES FOUR

INGREDIENTS
900ml/1½ pints/3¾ cups water
5ml/1 tsp salt
150g/5oz/generous 1 cup polenta
  or cornmeal
50g/2oz/⅓ cup freshly grated
  Parmesan cheese
5ml/1 tsp chopped fresh thyme
90ml/6 tbsp olive oil
675g/1½lb onions, halved and sliced
2 garlic cloves, chopped
a few fresh thyme sprigs
5ml/1 tsp brown sugar
15–30ml/1–2 tbsp balsamic vinegar
2 heads radicchio, cut into thick
  slices or wedges
225g/8oz Taleggio cheese, sliced
salt and ground black pepper

1 In a large pan, bring the water to the boil and add the salt. Adjust the heat so that it simmers. Stirring all the time, add the polenta in a steady stream, then bring to the boil. Cook over a very low heat, stirring frequently, for 30–40 minutes, until thick and smooth.

2 Beat in the Parmesan and chopped thyme, then turn on to a work surface or tray. Spread evenly, then leave to cool.

3 Heat 30ml/2 tbsp of the oil in a frying pan over a moderate heat. Add the onions and stir to coat in the oil, then cover and cook over a very low heat for 15 minutes, stirring occasionally.

4 Add the garlic and most of the thyme sprigs and cook, uncovered, for another 10 minutes, or until light brown.

5 Add the sugar, 15ml/1 tbsp of the vinegar and salt and pepper. Cook for another 5–10 minutes, until soft and well-browned. Taste and add more vinegar and seasoning as necessary.

6 Preheat the grill (broiler). Cut the polenta into thick slices and brush with a little of the remaining oil, then grill (broil) until crusty and lightly browned.

7 Turn the polenta and add the radicchio to the grill rack or pan. Season the radicchio and brush with a little oil. Grill for about 5 minutes, until the polenta and radicchio are browned. Drizzle a little vinegar over the radicchio.

8 Heap the onions on to the polenta. Scatter the cheese and a few sprigs of thyme over both polenta and radicchio. Grill until the cheese is bubbling. Season with pepper and serve immediately.

COOK'S TIP
If you cannot find raddichio, try chicory, and use red onions to add colour.

Energy 611kcal/2534kJ; Protein 22.7g; Carbohydrate 42.5g, of which sugars 11.2g; Fat 37.8g, of which saturates 15.3g; Cholesterol 65mg; Calcium 365mg; Fibre 4.1g; Sodium 457mg.

LAYERED POLENTA BAKE

THIS IS A FORM OF LASAGNE WITH SLICES OF POLENTA REPLACING THE USUAL SHEETS OF PASTA.
LAYERS OF POLENTA ARE INTERSPERSED WITH A RICH TOMATO SAUCE AND CREAMY GORGONZOLA.

SERVES SIX

INGREDIENTS
  5ml/1 tsp salt
  375g/13oz/3 cups fine polenta
  olive oil, for greasing and brushing
  25g/1oz/⅓ cup freshly grated
    Parmesan cheese
  salt and ground black pepper
For the tomato sauce
  15ml/1 tbsp olive oil
  2 garlic cloves, chopped
  400g/14oz/3 cups chopped tomatoes
  15ml/1 tbsp chopped fresh sage
  2.5ml/½ tsp soft brown sugar
  400g/14oz can cannellini beans,
    rinsed and drained
For the spinach sauce
  250g/9oz spinach, tough stalks
    removed
  150ml/¼ pint/⅔ cup single
    (light) cream
  115g/4oz/1 cup Gorgonzola
    cheese, cubed
  large pinch of ground nutmeg

1 Make the polenta. Bring 2 litres/
3½ pints/8 cups water to the boil
in a large heavy pan and add the
salt. Remove the pan from the heat.
Gradually pour in the polenta,
whisking continuously.

2 Return the pan to the heat and stir
constantly for 15–20 minutes until the
polenta is thick and comes away from
the side of the pan. Remove the pan
from the heat.

3 Season well with pepper, then spoon
the polenta on to a wet work surface or
piece of marble. Using a wet spatula,
spread out the polenta until it is
1cm/½in thick. Leave to cool for about
1 hour.

4 Preheat the oven to 190°C/375°F/
Gas 5. To make the tomato sauce, heat
the oil in a pan, then fry the garlic for
1 minute. Add the tomatoes and sage
and bring to the boil. Reduce the heat,
add the sugar and seasoning, and
simmer for 10 minutes until slightly
reduced, stirring occasionally. Stir in the
beans and cook for a further 2 minutes.

5 Meanwhile, wash the spinach
thoroughly and place in a large pan
with only the water that clings to the
leaves. Cover the pan tightly and cook
over a medium heat for about 3 minutes
or until tender, stirring occasionally.
Tip the spinach into a colander and
drain, then squeeze out as much excess
water as possible with the back of a
wooden spoon.

6 Heat the cream, cheese and nutmeg
in a heavy pan. Bring to the boil, then
reduce the heat. Stir in the spinach and
seasoning, then cook gently until
slightly thickened, stirring frequently.

7 Cut the polenta into triangles, then
place a layer in an oiled deep baking
dish. Spoon over the tomato sauce,
then top with another layer of polenta.
Top with the spinach sauce and cover
with the remaining polenta triangles.
Brush with olive oil, sprinkle with
Parmesan and bake for 35–40 minutes.
Heat the grill (broiler) to high and grill
(broil) until the top is golden. Serve.

Energy 436kcal/1820kJ; Protein 16.2g; Carbohydrate 55.3g, of which sugars 4.9g; Fat 16.3g, of which saturates 8g; Cholesterol 32mg; Calcium 267mg; Fibre 5g; Sodium 481mg.

BARLEY RISOTTO WITH ROASTED SQUASH

THIS RISOTTO IS MORE LIKE A PILAFF, MADE WITH SLIGHTLY CHEWY, NUTTY-FLAVOURED PEARL BARLEY, RATHER THAN THE RICE OF A CLASSIC ITALIAN RISOTTO. SWEET LEEKS AND ROASTED SQUASH ARE SUPERB WITH EARTHY BARLEY, AND THIS MAKES A GREAT MEAL FOR THE AUTUMN.

SERVES FOUR TO FIVE

INGREDIENTS

200g/7oz/1 cup pearl barley
1 butternut squash, peeled, seeded
  and cut into chunks
10ml/2 tsp chopped fresh thyme
60ml/4 tbsp olive oil
25g/1oz/2 tbsp butter
4 leeks, cut into fairly thick
  diagonal slices
2 garlic cloves, finely chopped
175g/6oz chestnut mushrooms, sliced
2 carrots, coarsely grated
about 120ml/4fl oz/½ cup
  vegetable stock
30ml/2 tbsp chopped fresh flat
  leaf parsley
50g/2oz Pecorino cheese, grated
  or shaved
45ml/3 tbsp pumpkin seeds, toasted,
  or chopped walnuts
salt and ground black pepper

1 Rinse the barley, then cook it in simmering water, keeping the pan part-covered, for 35–45 minutes, or until tender. Drain. Preheat the oven to 200°C/400°F/Gas 6.

2 Place the squash in a roasting pan with half the thyme. Season with pepper and toss with half the oil. Roast, stirring once, for 30–35 minutes, until tender and beginning to brown.

3 Heat half the butter with the remaining oil in a large pan. Cook the leeks and garlic gently for 5 minutes.

4 Add the mushrooms and remaining thyme, then cook until the liquid from the mushrooms evaporates and they begin to fry.

5 Stir in the carrots and cook for 2 minutes, then add the barley and most of the stock. Season well and part-cover the pan. Cook for a further 5 minutes. Pour in the remaining stock if the mixture seems dry.

6 Stir in the parsley, the remaining butter and half the Pecorino, then stir in the squash. Add seasoning to taste and serve immediately, sprinkled with the toasted pumpkin seeds or walnuts and the remaining Pecorino.

Energy 409kcal/1713kJ; Protein 11.8g; Carbohydrate 43.4g, of which sugars 7.1g; Fat 22.1g, of which saturates 6.6g; Cholesterol 21mg; Calcium 249mg; Fibre 4.9g; Sodium 159mg.

RED ONION TART WITH A CORNMEAL CRUST

WONDERFULLY MILD AND SWEET WHEN COOKED, RED ONIONS GO WELL WITH FONTINA CHEESE AND THYME IN THIS TART. CORNMEAL GIVES THE PASTRY A CRUMBLY TEXTURE TO CONTRAST WITH THE JUICINESS OF THE ONION FILLING. A TOMATO AND BASIL SALAD IS GOOD WITH THE TART.

SERVES FIVE TO SIX

INGREDIENTS
    60ml/4 tbsp olive oil
    1kg/2¼lb red onions, thinly sliced
    2–3 garlic cloves, thinly sliced
    5ml/1 tsp chopped fresh thyme, plus
      a few whole sprigs
    5ml/1 tsp dark brown sugar
    10ml/2 tsp sherry vinegar
    225g/8oz Fontina cheese,
      thinly sliced
    salt and ground black pepper
For the pastry
    115g/4oz/1 cup plain (all-purpose)
      flour
    75g/3oz/¾ cup fine yellow cornmeal
    5ml/1 tsp dark brown sugar
    5ml/1 tsp chopped fresh thyme
    90g/3½oz/7 tbsp butter
    1 egg yolk
    30–45ml/2–3 tbsp iced water

1 To make the pastry, sift the flour and cornmeal into a bowl with 5ml/1 tsp salt. Add black pepper and stir in the sugar and thyme. Rub in the butter until the mixture looks like breadcrumbs. Beat the egg yolk with 30ml/2 tbsp of the iced water and use to bind the pastry, adding the remaining water if necessary. Gather the dough into a ball, wrap in clear film (plastic wrap) and chill it for 30–40 minutes.

2 Heat 45ml/3 tbsp of the oil in a deep frying pan and add the onions. Cover and cook slowly, stirring occasionally, for 20–30 minutes.

3 Add the garlic and chopped thyme, then cook, stirring occasionally, for another 10 minutes. Increase the heat slightly, then add the sugar and sherry vinegar. Cook, uncovered, for another 5–6 minutes, until the onions start to caramelize slightly. Season to taste with salt and pepper.

4 Preheat the oven to 190°C/375°F/ Gas 5. Roll out the pastry thinly and use to line a 25cm/10in loose-base metal flan tin (pan).

5 Prick the pastry all over with a fork and support the sides with foil. Bake for 12–15 minutes, until lightly coloured.

6 Remove the foil and spread the caramelized onions evenly over the base of the pastry case. Add the slices of Fontina and sprigs of thyme, and season with pepper. Drizzle over the remaining oil, then bake for 15–20 minutes, until the filling is piping hot and the cheese is beginning to bubble. Garnish the tart with thyme and serve.

Energy 494kcal/2051kJ; Protein 13.2g; Carbohydrate 38.9g, of which sugars 11.3g; Fat 31.7g, of which saturates 16g; Cholesterol 100mg; Calcium 172mg; Fibre 3.2g; Sodium 307mg.

VEGETABLE AND EGG NOODLE RIBBONS

SERVE THIS COLOURFUL NOODLE DISH AS A LIGHT LUNCH OR SERVE IN SMALLER PORTIONS FOR A STARTER. IT'S IDEAL FOR THE SUMMER, WHEN YOU MAY ALSO USE FRESHLY SHELLED PEAS.

SERVES FOUR

INGREDIENTS
1 large carrot, peeled
2 courgettes (zucchini)
50g/2oz/4 tbsp butter
15ml/1 tbsp olive oil
6 fresh shiitake mushrooms,
  finely sliced
50g/2oz/½ cup frozen peas, thawed
350g/12oz thick egg noodles
10ml/2 tsp chopped mixed fresh
  herbs such as marjoram, chives
  and basil
salt and ground black pepper
25g/1oz Parmesan cheese, to serve
  (optional)

1 Slice thin strips from the carrot and from the courgettes.

2 Heat the butter with the olive oil in a frying pan. Stir in the carrots and mushrooms; fry for 2 minutes. Add the courgettes and peas and stir-fry until the courgettes are cooked. Season.

3 Meanwhile, cook the noodles in a large pan of boiling water. Drain and tip them into a bowl. Add the vegetables and toss to mix.

4 Sprinkle over the mixed herbs and season to taste. If using the Parmesan cheese, grate it over the top.

Energy 496kcal/2082kJ; Protein 13.5g; Carbohydrate 67.7g, of which sugars 5.2g; Fat 20.9g, of which saturates 9.1g; Cholesterol 53mg; Calcium 56mg; Fibre 4.7g; Sodium 242mg.

BUCKWHEAT NOODLES WITH GOAT'S CHEESE

WHEN YOU DON'T FEEL LIKE DOING A LOT OF COOKING, TRY THIS GOOD, FAST SUPPER DISH. THE EARTHY FLAVOUR OF BUCKWHEAT GOES WELL WITH THE NUTTY, PEPPERY TASTE OF ROCKET LEAVES, OFFSET BY THE DELICIOUSLY CREAMY GOAT'S CHEESE.

SERVES FOUR

INGREDIENTS
350g/12oz buckwheat noodles
50g/2oz/4 tbsp butter
2 garlic cloves, finely chopped
4 shallots, sliced
75g/3oz/1½ cups hazelnuts, lightly
  roasted and roughly chopped
large handful rocket (arugula) leaves
175g/6oz goat's cheese
salt and ground black pepper

1 Cook the noodles in a large pan of boiling water until just tender. Drain well.

2 Heat the butter in a large frying pan. Add the garlic and shallots and cook for 2–3 minutes, stirring all the time, until the shallots are soft.

3 Add the hazelnuts and fry for about 1 minute. Add the rocket leaves and, when they start to wilt, toss in the noodles and heat through.

4 Season with salt and pepper. Crumble in the goat's cheese and serve immediately.

COOK'S TIP
Long pasta, such as spaghetti, linguine or tagliatelle, would also work well in this recipe.

Energy 700kcal/2930kJ; Protein 22.4g; Carbohydrate 69.4g, of which sugars 4.2g; Fat 38.9g, of which saturates 15.2g; Cholesterol 67mg; Calcium 111mg; Fibre 4g; Sodium 342mg.

POULTRY, MEAT AND FISH

*In the past, grains were used to eke out the meat
or poultry content in dishes that have now
become firm favourites in restaurants and home
kitchens alike, such as Chicken and Asparagus
Risotto or Tagliatelli with Bolognese Sauce.
The firm bite of grains with delicate fish is also
delicious, and recipes include Trout Cannelloni,
Red Rice Salad Niçoise and Seafood Paella.*

ALICANTE CRUSTED RICE

*PAELLA CON COSTRA IS AN UNUSUAL PAELLA WITH AN EGG CRUST THAT IS FINISHED IN THE OVEN.
THE CRUST SEALS IN ALL THE AROMAS UNTIL IT IS BROKEN OPEN AT THE TABLE.*

SERVES SIX

INGREDIENTS
  45ml/3 tbsp olive oil
  200g/7oz *butifarra*, fresh sausages
  or frying chorizo, sliced
  2 tomatoes, peeled, seeded
  and chopped
  175g/6oz lean cubed pork
  175g/6oz skinless, boneless chicken
  breast or rabbit, cut into chunks
  350g/12oz/1¾ cups paella rice
  900ml–1 litre/1½–1¾ pints/
  3¾–4 cups hot chicken stock
  pinch of saffron threads (0.2g)
  150g/5oz/⅔ cup cooked chickpeas
  6 large (US extra large) eggs
  salt and ground black pepper

1 Preheat the oven to 190°C/375°F/
Gas 5. Heat the oil in a flameproof
casserole and fry the sausage until
browned. Add the tomatoes and fry until
reduced. Stir in the pork and chicken or
rabbit pieces and cook for 2–3 minutes
until the meat has browned lightly, stirring.

2 Add the rice to the pan, stir over the
heat for about 1 minute, then pour in
the hot stock. Add the saffron, season
to taste, and stir well.

3 Bring to the boil, then lower the heat
and add the chickpeas. Cover the
casserole tightly with the lid and cook
over a low heat for about 20 minutes or
until the rice is tender.

4 Beat the eggs with a little water and a
pinch of salt and pour over the rice.
Place the casserole, uncovered, in the
oven and cook for about 10 minutes,
until the eggs have set and browned
slightly on top. Serve the paella straight
from the casserole.

Energy 533kcal/2226kJ; Protein 29.1g; Carbohydrate 55.5g, of which sugars 1.7g; Fat 21.7g, of which saturates 6.3g; Cholesterol 242mg; Calcium 72mg; Fibre 1.5g; Sodium 436mg.

CHICKEN AND ASPARAGUS RISOTTO

USE THICK SPEARS OF LOCAL, SEASONAL ASPARAGUS FOR THIS RISOTTO, AS IT IS FULL OF FLAVOUR AND BECOMES BEAUTIFULLY TENDER IN THE TIME IT TAKES FOR THE RICE TO ABSORB THE STOCK.

SERVES FOUR

INGREDIENTS

75ml/5 tbsp olive oil
1 leek, finely chopped
115g/4oz/1½ cups oyster or brown cap (cremini) mushrooms, sliced
3 skinless, boneless chicken breast fillets, cubed
350g/12oz asparagus
250g/9oz/1¼ cups risotto rice
900ml/1½ pints/3¾ cups simmering chicken stock
sea salt and ground black pepper
fresh Parmesan shavings, to serve

1 Heat the olive oil in a pan. Add the finely chopped leek and cook gently until softened, but not coloured. Add the sliced mushrooms and cook for 5 minutes. Remove the vegetables from the pan and set aside.

2 Increase the heat and cook the cubes of chicken until golden on all sides. Do this in batches, if necessary, and then return them all to the pan.

3 Meanwhile, discard the woody ends from the asparagus and cut the spears in half. Set the tips aside. Cut the thick ends in half and add them to the pan. Return the leek and mushroom mixture to the pan and stir in the rice.

4 Pour in a ladleful of boiling stock and cook gently, stirring occasionally, until the stock is completely absorbed. Continue adding the stock a ladleful at a time, simmering until it is absorbed, the rice is tender and the chicken is cooked.

COOK'S TIP
To thoroughly remove all the soil from leeks, slice them in half along their length and rinse under running water.

5 Add the asparagus tips with the last ladleful of boiling stock for the final 5 minutes and continue cooking the risotto very gently until the asparagus is tender. The whole process should take about 25–30 minutes.

6 Season the risotto to taste with salt and freshly ground black pepper and spoon it into individual warm serving bowls. Top each bowl with curls of cheese, and serve.

Energy 496kcal/2072kJ; Protein 36.1g; Carbohydrate 50g, of which sugars 2.7g; Fat 16.1g, of which saturates 7.4g; Cholesterol 105mg; Calcium 53mg; Fibre 2.7g; Sodium 148mg.

PAN-FRIED PHEASANT WITH OATMEAL

OATS ARE A LOVELY COATING FOR POULTRY, GAME AND OTHER MEATS. SWEET, SLIGHTLY TANGY REDCURRANT JELLY IS USED TO BIND THE OATMEAL TO THE TENDER PHEASANT BREAST FILLETS.

SERVES FOUR

INGREDIENTS

115g/4oz/generous 1 cup medium
  rolled oats
4 skinless, boneless pheasant breasts
45ml/3 tbsp redcurrant jelly, melted
50g/2oz/¼ cup butter
15ml/1 tbsp olive oil
45ml/3 tbsp wholegrain mustard
300ml/½ pint/1¼ cups double
  (heavy) cream
salt and ground black pepper

1 Place the rolled oats on a plate and season with salt and ground black pepper. Brush the skinned pheasant breasts with the melted redcurrant jelly, then turn them in the oats to coat evenly. Shake off any excess oats and set aside.

2 Heat the butter and oil in a frying pan until foaming. Add the pheasant breasts and cook over a high heat, turning frequently, until they are golden brown on all sides. Reduce the heat to medium and cook for a further 8–10 minutes, turning once or twice, until the meat is thoroughly cooked.

3 Add the mustard and cream, stirring to combine with the cooking juices. Bring slowly to the boil then simmer for 10 minutes over a low heat, or until the sauce has thickened to a good consistency. Serve immediately.

Energy 847kcal/3520kJ; Protein 37.1g; Carbohydrate 30.1g, of which sugars 9.1g; Fat 59g, of which saturates 35.1g; Cholesterol 129mg; Calcium 105mg; Fibre 2g; Sodium 205mg.

PORK EMPANADA

THIS IS A FLAT, TWO-CRUST GALICIAN PIE MADE USING A CORNMEAL DOUGH. FILLINGS VARY
ENORMOUSLY, AND MAY INCLUDE FISH SUCH AS SARDINES, OR SCALLOPS FOR SPECIAL OCCASIONS.

SERVES EIGHT

INGREDIENTS
  75ml/5 tbsp olive oil
  2 onions, chopped
  4 garlic cloves, finely chopped
  1kg/2¼lb boneless pork loin, diced
  175g/6oz smoked gammon (smoked
    or cured ham) or raw ham, diced
  3 red chorizo or other spicy sausages
    (about 300g/11oz)
  3 (bell) peppers (mixed colours),
    seeded and chopped
  175ml/6fl oz/¾ cup white wine
  200g/7oz can tomatoes
  pinch of saffron threads
  5ml/1 tsp paprika
  30ml/2 tbsp chopped fresh parsley
  salt and ground black pepper
For the cornmeal dough
  250g/9oz/2¼ cups cornmeal
  7g/2 tsp easy-blend (rapid-rise)
    dried yeast
  5ml/1 tsp caster (superfine) sugar
  250g/9oz/2¼ cups plain
    (all-purpose) flour, plus extra for
    dusting
  5ml/1 tsp salt
  200ml/7fl oz/scant 1 cup warm water
  30ml/2 tbsp oil
  2 eggs, beaten, plus 1 for the glaze

1 Make the filling. Heat 60ml/4 tbsp oil
in a frying pan and fry the onions,
adding the garlic when the onions begin
to colour. Transfer to a flameproof
casserole. Add the pork and gammon or
ham to the pan, and fry until coloured,
stirring. Transfer to the casserole.

2 Add the remaining oil, the sausage
and peppers to the pan and fry.
Transfer to the casserole. Deglaze the
pan with the wine, allowing it to bubble
and reduce. Pour into the casserole.

COOK'S TIP
You could make this pie with chicken
and turkey instead of the pork. If using
poultry, use smoked paprika instead of
regular paprika for extra flavour.

3 Add the tomatoes, saffron, paprika
and parsley and season. Cook gently
for 20–30 minutes. Leave to cool.

4 Meanwhile make the dough. Mix the
cornmeal, dried yeast, sugar, flour and
salt in a food processor. Pulse to mix.
Gradually add the water, oil and 2 eggs
with the motor running, to make a
smooth soft dough.

5 Turn the dough into a clean bowl,
cover with a dish towel and leave in a
warm place for 40–50 minutes, to rise.

6 Preheat the oven to 200°C/400°F/
Gas 6. Grease a shallow roasting pan
or dish 30 × 20cm/12 × 8in. Halve the
dough. Roll out one half on a floured
surface, a little larger than the pan. Lift
this in place, leaving the border hanging
over the edge.

7 Spoon in the filling. Roll out the lid
and arrange it in place. Fold the outside
edge over the lid (trimming as
necessary) and press gently all round
with a fork, to seal the pie. Prick the
surface and brush with beaten egg.

8 Bake the pie for 30–35 minutes. Cut
the pie into squares.

Energy 649kcal/2717kJ; Protein 44.8g; Carbohydrate 59.6g, of which sugars 9.7g; Fat 24.9g, of which saturates 5.9g; Cholesterol 182mg; Calcium 92mg; Fibre 4g; Sodium 680mg.

PANCETTA AND BROAD BEAN RISOTTO

THIS DELICIOUS RISOTTO MAKES A HEALTHY AND FILLING MEAL WHEN SERVED WITH A MIXED GREEN SALAD. USE SMOKED BACON INSTEAD OF PANCETTA, IF YOU LIKE.

SERVES FOUR

INGREDIENTS

   225g/8oz frozen baby broad
     (fava) beans
   15ml/1 tbsp olive oil
   1 onion, chopped
   2 garlic cloves, finely chopped
   175g/6oz smoked pancetta, diced
   350g/12oz/1¾ cups risotto rice
   1.2 litres/2 pints/5 cups
     simmering chicken stock
   30ml/2 tbsp chopped fresh mixed
     herbs, such as parsley, thyme
     and oregano
   salt and ground black pepper
   coarsely chopped fresh parsley,
     to garnish
   shavings of Parmesan cheese,
     to serve (see Cook's Tip)

1 First, cook the broad beans in a large pan of lightly salted boiling water for about 3 minutes until tender. Drain and set aside.

COOK'S TIP
To make thin Parmesan cheese shavings, take a rectangular block or long wedge of Parmesan and firmly scrape a vegetable peeler down the side of the cheese to make shavings. The swivel-bladed type of peeler is best for this job.

2 Heat the olive oil in a flameproof casserole. Add the chopped onion, chopped garlic and diced pancetta, and cook gently for about 5 minutes, stirring occasionally.

3 Add the rice to the casserole and cook for 1 minute, stirring. Add 300ml/ ½ pint/1¼ cups of the stock and simmer, stirring frequently until it has been absorbed.

4 Continue adding the stock, a ladleful at a time, stirring frequently until the rice is just tender and creamy, and almost all of the liquid has been absorbed. This will take 30–35 minutes. It may not be necessary to add all the stock.

5 Stir the beans, mixed herbs and seasoning into the risotto. Heat gently, then serve garnished with the chopped fresh parsley and sprinkled with shavings of Parmesan cheese.

Energy 511Kcal/2132kJ; Protein 18g; Carbohydrate 77.6g, of which sugars 1.6g; Fat 13.9g, of which saturates 4g; Cholesterol 28mg; Calcium 55mg; Fibre 3.9g; Sodium 556mg.

LAMB AND CARROT CASSEROLE WITH BARLEY

BARLEY AND CARROTS MAKE NATURAL PARTNERS FOR LAMB OR MUTTON. THE BARLEY ADDS FLAVOUR AND TEXTURE AS WELL AS THICKENING THE SAUCE, WHICH IS DELICIOUS MOPPED UP WITH BREAD.

SERVES SIX

INGREDIENTS

675g/1½lb boneless lamb
15ml/1 tbsp vegetable oil
2 onions
675g/1½lb carrots, thickly sliced
4–6 celery sticks, sliced
45ml/3 tbsp pearl barley, rinsed
600ml/1 pint/2½ cups near-boiling
  lamb or vegetable stock
5ml/1 tsp fresh thyme leaves or
  pinch of dried mixed herbs
salt and ground black pepper
spring cabbage and baked potatoes,
  to serve

1 Preheat the oven to 160°C/325°F/Gas 3. Trim the lamb. Cut the meat into 3cm/1¼in pieces. Heat the oil in a frying pan, add the lamb and fry until browned. Remove with a slotted spoon and set aside.

2 Slice the onions and add to the pan. Fry gently for 5 minutes. Add the carrots and celery and cook for 3–4 minutes. Transfer to a casserole.

3 Sprinkle the pearl barley over the vegetables in the casserole, then arrange the lamb pieces on top.

4 Lightly season with salt and ground black pepper, then scatter with the herbs. Pour the stock over the meat, so that all of the meat is covered.

5 Cover the casserole with the lid and cook in the oven for about 2 hours or until the meat, vegetables and barley are tender.

6 Taste and adjust the seasoning before serving with spring cabbage and baked potatoes.

Energy 310kcal/1295kJ; Protein 24.2g; Carbohydrate 20.6g, of which sugars 12.2g; Fat 15.1g, of which saturates 6.2g; Cholesterol 86mg; Calcium 64mg; Fibre 3.9g; Sodium 139mg.

LAMB AND PUMPKIN COUSCOUS

PUMPKIN IS A VERY POPULAR MOROCCAN INGREDIENT AND THIS IS A TRADITIONAL COUSCOUS RECIPE, WITH ECHOES OF THE VERY EARLY VEGETABLE COUSCOUS DISHES MADE BY THE BERBERS.

2 Cut the lamb into bitesize pieces and place in the pan with the sliced onions, and add the saffron, ginger, turmeric, pepper and salt. Pour in the water and stir well, then slowly bring to the boil. Cover the pan and simmer for about 1 hour or until the meat is tender.

3 Peel or scrape the carrots and cut them into large chunks. Cut the pumpkin into 2.5cm/1in cubes, discarding the skin, seeds and pith.

4 Stir the carrots, pumpkin and raisins into the meat mixture with the chickpeas, cover the pan and simmer for 30–35 minutes more, stirring occasionally, until the vegetables and meat are completely tender.

5 Meanwhile, prepare the couscous according to the instructions on the packet, and steam on top of the stew, then fork lightly to fluff up. Spoon the couscous on to a warmed serving plate, add the stew and stir the stew into the couscous. Extra gravy can be served separately. Sprinkle some tiny sprigs of fresh parsley over the top and serve immediately.

SERVES FOUR TO SIX

INGREDIENTS
75g/3oz/½ cup chickpeas, soaked
  overnight and drained
675g/1½lb lean lamb
2 large onions, sliced
pinch of saffron threads
1.5ml/¼ tsp ground ginger
2.5ml/½ tsp ground turmeric
5ml/1 tsp ground black pepper
1.2 litres/2 pints/5 cups water
450g/1lb carrots
675g/1½lb pumpkin
75g/3oz/⅔ cup raisins
400g/14oz/2¼ cups couscous
salt
sprigs of fresh parsley, to garnish

1 Place the chickpeas in a large pan of boiling water. Boil for 10 minutes, then reduce the heat and cook for 1–1½ hours until tender. Drain and place in cold water. Remove the skins by rubbing with your fingers. Discard the skins and drain.

Energy 725Kcal/3034kJ; Protein 34.8g; Carbohydrate 115.4g, of which sugars 69.5g; Fat 16.6g, of which saturates 6.8g; Cholesterol 86mg; Calcium 282mg; Fibre 21.5g; Sodium 297mg.

CHOLENT

THIS IS AN ESSENTIAL DISH IN JEWISH CUISINE. BEANS, RICE AND BARLEY, MEAT, SWEET VEGETABLES AND WHOLE BOILED EGGS MAKE A BEAUTIFULLY BALANCED AND DELICIOUS CASSEROLE.

SERVES FOUR

INGREDIENTS

250g/9oz/1⅓ cups dried haricot (navy) beans
30ml/2 tbsp olive oil
1 onion, chopped
4 garlic cloves, finely chopped
50g/2oz/1¼ cups pearl barley
15ml/1 tbsp ground paprika
pinch of cayenne pepper
1 celery stick, chopped
400g/14oz can chopped tomatoes
3 carrots, sliced
1 small turnip, diced
2 baking potatoes, peeled and cut into chunks
675g/1½lb mixture of beef brisket, stewing beef and smoked beef, cut into cubes
1 litre/1¾ pints/4 cups boiling beef stock
30ml/2 tbsp easy-cook (converted) white rice
4 eggs, at room temperature
salt and ground black pepper

3 Preheat the oven to 160°C/325°F/Gas 3. Meanwhile, heat the oil in a pan, add the onion and garlic, and cook gently for about 10 minutes, or until soft. Transfer to a large casserole.

4 Add the beans, barley, paprika, cayenne, celery, tomatoes, carrots, turnip and potatoes to the onion. Mix well and place the meats on top.

5 Cover and cook in the oven for 3 hours, or until the meat and vegetables are very tender. Add the rice, stir, and season with salt and pepper.

6 Rinse the eggs in tepid water, then lower them, one at a time, into the casserole. Cover and cook for a further 45 minutes, or until the rice is cooked. Serve hot, making sure each portion contains a whole egg.

1 Place the beans in a large bowl. Pour over plenty of cold water to cover and leave to soak for at least 8 hours, or overnight if you like.

2 Drain the beans well, then place them in a large pan, cover with fresh cold water and bring to the boil. Boil them steadily for about 10 minutes, skimming off any froth that rises to the surface, then drain well and set aside.

Energy 860Kcal/3607kJ; Protein 58.9g; Carbohydrate 74.2g, of which sugars 13.7g; Fat 38.8g, of which saturates 12.7g; Cholesterol 341mg; Calcium 164mg; Fibre 10.9g; Sodium 639mg.

PAPPARDELLE WITH RABBIT SAUCE

THIS DISH COMES FROM THE NORTH OF ITALY, WHERE RABBIT SAUCES FOR PASTA ARE VERY POPULAR. IF MAKING YOUR OWN PAPPARDELLE USE SPINACH OR WHOLEMEAL FLOUR FOR A HEALTHIER DISH.

SERVES FOUR

INGREDIENTS

15g/½oz dried porcini mushrooms
175ml/6fl oz/¾ cup warm water
1 small onion
½ carrot
½ celery stick
2 bay leaves
25g/1oz/2 tbsp butter
15ml/1 tbsp olive oil
40g/1½oz pancetta or rindless
  streaky bacon, chopped
15ml/1 tbsp roughly chopped fresh
  flat leaf parsley, plus extra
  to garnish
250g/9oz boneless rabbit meat
90ml/6 tbsp dry white wine
200g/7oz can chopped Italian plum
  tomatoes or 200ml/7fl oz/scant
  1 cup passata
300g/11oz fresh or dried pappardelle
salt and ground black pepper

1 Put the dried mushrooms in a bowl, pour over the warm water and leave to soak for 15–20 minutes. Finely chop the vegetables, either in a food processor or by hand. Make a tear in each bay leaf, so that they will release their flavour when added to the sauce.

2 Heat the butter and oil in a skillet or medium saucepan until just sizzling. Add the chopped vegetables, pancetta or bacon and the parsley and cook for about 5 minutes.

3 Add the pieces of rabbit and fry on both sides for 3–4 minutes. Pour the wine over and let it reduce for a few minutes, then add the tomatoes or passata. Drain the mushrooms and pour the soaking liquid into the pan. Chop the mushrooms and add them to the mixture, with the bay leaves and salt and pepper to taste. Stir well, cover and simmer for 35–40 minutes until the rabbit is tender, stirring occasionally.

4 Remove the pan from the heat and lift out the pieces of rabbit with a slotted spoon. Cut them into bite-size chunks and stir them into the sauce. Remove and discard the bay leaves. Taste the sauce and add more salt and pepper, if needed.Cook the pasta according to the instructions on the packet. Meanwhile, reheat the sauce. Drain the pasta and toss with the sauce in a warmed bowl. Serve immediately, sprinkled with parsley.

Energy 465kcal/1961kJ; Protein 24.9g; Carbohydrate 59.3g, of which sugars 5.8g; Fat 14.3g, of which saturates 5.7g; Cholesterol 64mg; Calcium 48mg; Fibre 3.2g; Sodium 219mg.

TAGLIATELLE BOLOGNESE

*THIS IS THE CLASSIC PASTA DISH, A FAVOURITE WITH CHILDREN AND ADULTS ALIKE. FRESH PASTA
WORKS VERY WELL, BUT USE DRIED TAGLIATELLE NESTS OR SPAGHETTI FOR CONVENIENCE.*

SERVES FOUR TO SIX

INGREDIENTS
1 onion
1 small carrot
1 celery stick
2 garlic cloves
45ml/3 tbsp olive oil
400g/14oz minced (ground) beef
120ml/4fl oz/1/2 cup red wine
200ml/7fl oz/scant 1 cup passata
(bottled strained tomatoes)
15ml/1 tbsp tomato purée (paste)
5ml/1 tsp dried oregano
15ml/1 tbsp chopped fresh flat leaf
parsley
about 350ml/12fl oz/11/2 cups beef
stock
8 baby Italian tomatoes (optional)
300g/11oz fresh or dried tagliatelli
salt and ground black pepper

COOK'S TIP
Although Spaghetti Bolognese is famous,
tagliatelle is actually the authentic pasta
to eat with Bolognese sauce. Tagliatelle
is one of the easiest pasta shapes to
make at home.

1 Chop all the vegetables finely, either
in a food processor or by hand. Heat
the oil in a large pan, add the chopped
vegetable mixture and cook over a low
heat, stirring frequently, for 5–7
minutes.

2 Add the minced beef and cook for
5 minutes, stirring frequently and
breaking up any lumps in the meat with
a wooden spoon. Stir in the wine and
mix well.

3 Cook for 1–2 minutes, then add the
passata, tomato purée, herbs and
60ml/4 tbsp of the stock. Season with
salt and pepper to taste. Stir well and
bring to the boil.

4 Cover the pan, and cook over a
gentle heat for 30 minutes, stirring
from time to time and adding more
stock as necessary. Add the tomatoes,
if using, and simmer for 5–10 minutes
more. Taste for seasoning.

5 Bring a large pan of lightly salted
water to the boil. Add a few drops of
olive oil (to prevent sticking) and add
the fresh or dried pasta, cooking
according to the packet instructions.
Drain well in a colander, rinse with
fresh boiled water and drain again.
Toss the Bolognese sauce into the
pasta and serve at once.

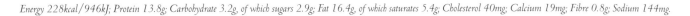

Energy 228kcal/946kJ; Protein 13.8g; Carbohydrate 3.2g, of which sugars 2.9g; Fat 16.4g, of which saturates 5.4g; Cholesterol 40mg; Calcium 19mg; Fibre 0.8g; Sodium 144mg.

BUCKWHEAT NOODLES <u>WITH</u> SMOKED SALMON

JAPANESE SOBA OR BUCKWHEAT NOODLES HAVE A DELICIOUS, SLIGHTLY EARTHY FLAVOUR. THE SALMON COOKS AS YOU WORK IT INTO THE WARM, FRAGRANT NOODLES, AND THE CHIVES GIVE AN EXTRA BITE.

SERVES FOUR

INGREDIENTS
  225g/8oz buckwheat or soba noodles
  15ml/1 tbsp oyster sauce
  juice of ½ lemon
  30–45ml/2–3 tbsp light olive oil
  115g/4oz smoked salmon, cut into
    fine strips
  115g/4oz young pea sprouts
  2 ripe tomatoes, peeled, seeded and
    cut into strips
  15ml/1 tbsp chopped chives
  ground black pepper

COOK'S TIP
Young pea sprouts are available for only
a short time. Use rocket (arugula)
instead if you cannot find them.

1 Cook the buckwheat or soba noodles
in a large pan of boiling water until
tender, following the directions on the
packet. Drain, then rinse under cold
running water and drain well.

2 Place the noodles in a large bowl.
Add the oyster sauce and lemon juice,
and season with pepper to taste.
Moisten the noodles with the olive oil.

3 Add the smoked salmon, pea
sprouts, tomatoes and chives. Mix well
and serve at once.

Energy 343kcal/1443kJ; Protein 16.3g; Carbohydrate 47.9g, of which sugars 3.8g; Fat 10.9g, of which saturates 1.2g; Cholesterol 10mg; Calcium 29mg; Fibre 3.5g; Sodium 814mg.

SEAFOOD PAELLA

PAELLA IS DESERVEDLY ONE OF SPAIN'S MOST FAMOUS DISHES. IN THIS LUXURIOUS VERSION, FLUFFY, SAFFRON-INFUSED RICE AND SUCCULENT SEAFOOD IS ENHANCED WITH SMOKY CHORIZO.

SERVES FOUR

INGREDIENTS

45ml/3 tbsp olive oil
1 Spanish (Bermuda) onion, chopped
2 fat garlic cloves, chopped
150g/5oz chorizo sausage, sliced
300g/11oz small squid, cleaned
1 red (bell) pepper, cut into strips
4 tomatoes, peeled, seeded and
  diced, or 200g/7oz can tomatoes
500ml/17fl oz/generous 2 cups
  chicken stock
105ml/7 tbsp dry white wine
200g/7oz/1 cup short grain Spanish
  paella rice
a large pinch of saffron threads
150g/5oz/1 cup fresh or frozen peas
12 large cooked prawns (shrimp), in
  the shell, or 8 langoustines
450g/1lb fresh mussels, scrubbed
450g/1lb medium clams, scrubbed
salt and ground black pepper

1 Heat the olive oil in a paella pan or wok, add the onion and garlic and fry until translucent. Add the chorizo and fry until lightly golden.

2 If the squid are very small, leave them whole, otherwise cut the bodies into rings and the tentacles into pieces. Add the squid to the pan and sauté over a high heat for 2 minutes.

3 Stir in the pepper strips and tomatoes, and simmer gently for 5 minutes, until the pepper strips are tender. Pour in the stock and wine, stir well and bring to the boil.

4 Stir in the rice and saffron threads and season well with salt and pepper. Spread the contents of the pan evenly. Bring the liquid back to the boil, then lower the heat and simmer gently for about 10 minutes.

5 Add the peas, prawns or langoustines, mussels and clams, stirring them gently into the rice.

6 Cook the paella gently for a further 15–20 minutes, until the rice is tender and all the mussels and clams have opened. If any remain closed, discard them. If the paella seems dry, add a little more hot chicken stock. Gently stir everything together and serve piping hot.

Energy 593kcal/2481kJ; Protein 43.1g; Carbohydrate 60.7g, of which sugars 11.2g; Fat 18.3g, of which saturates 3.9g; Cholesterol 308mg; Calcium 192mg; Fibre 4.6g; Sodium 1115mg.

TROUT WITH BLACK RICE

PINK TROUT FILLETS COOKED WITH GINGER, GARLIC AND CHILLI MAKE A STUNNING CONTRAST TO THE NUTTY BLACK RICE — A HEALTHY AND DELICIOUS GRAIN.

3 While the rice is cooking, preheat the oven to 200°C/400°F/Gas 6. In a small bowl mix together the grated ginger, garlic, chilli and soy sauce.

4 Place the fish, skin-side up, in a lightly oiled shallow baking dish. Using a sharp knife, make several slits in the skin of the fish, then spread the ginger paste all over the fillets.

5 Cover the dish tightly with foil and cook in the oven for 20–25 minutes or until the trout fillets are cooked through.

SERVES TWO

INGREDIENTS
   2.5cm/1in piece fresh root ginger,
     peeled and grated
   1 garlic clove, crushed
   1 fresh red chilli, seeded and
     finely chopped
   30ml/2 tbsp soy sauce
   2 trout fillets, each about 200g/7oz
   oil, for greasing
For the rice
   15ml/1 tbsp sesame oil
   50g/2oz/¾ cup fresh shiitake
     mushrooms, sliced
   8 spring onions (scallions),
     finely chopped
   150g/5oz/¾ cup black rice
   4 slices fresh root ginger
   900ml/1½ pints/3¾ cups
     boiling water

1 Make the rice. Heat the sesame oil in a pan and fry the mushrooms with half the spring onions for 2–3 minutes.

2 Add the rice and sliced ginger to the pan and stir well. Cover with the boiling water and bring to the boil. Reduce the heat, cover and simmer for 25–30 minutes or until the rice is tender. Drain well and cover to keep warm.

6 Divide the rice between two warmed serving plates. Remove the ginger. Lay the fish on top and sprinkle over the reserved spring onions, to garnish.

Energy 560kcal/2362kJ; Protein 45.6g; Carbohydrate 63.5g, of which sugars 3.3g; Fat 15.5g, of which saturates 1.4g; Cholesterol 0mg; Calcium 46mg; Fibre 2.3g; Sodium 1187mg.

RED RICE SALAD NIÇOISE

WITH ITS SWEET NUTTINESS, RED RICE GOES WELL IN THIS CLASSIC SALAD. THE TUNA OR SWORDFISH COULD BE BARBECUED OR PAN-FRIED BUT TAKE CARE NOT TO OVERCOOK IT.

SERVES SIX

INGREDIENTS
    about 675g/1½lb fresh tuna or
        swordfish, sliced into 2cm/¾in
        thick steaks
    350g/12oz/1¾ cups Camargue
        red rice
    fish or vegetable stock or water
    450g/1lb green beans
    450g/1lb broad (fava) beans, shelled
    1 Romaine lettuce
    450g/1lb cherry tomatoes, halved
        unless tiny
    30ml/2 tbsp coarsely chopped fresh
        coriander (cilantro)
    3 hard-boiled eggs
    175g/6oz/1½ cups pitted
        black olives
    olive oil, for brushing
For the marinade
    1 red onion, roughly chopped
    2 garlic cloves
    ½ bunch fresh parsley
    ½ bunch fresh coriander (cilantro)
    10ml/2 tsp paprika
    45ml/3 tbsp olive oil
    45ml/3 tbsp water
    30ml/2 tbsp white wine vinegar
    15ml/1 tbsp fresh lime or
        lemon juice
    salt and ground black pepper
For the dressing
    30ml/2 tbsp fresh lime or
        lemon juice
    3ml/1 tsp Dijon mustard
    ½ garlic clove, crushed (optional)
    60ml/4 tbsp olive oil
    60ml/4 tbsp sunflower oil

1 Make the marinade by mixing all the ingredients in a food processor and processing them for 30–40 seconds until the vegetables and herbs are finely chopped.

COOK'S TIP
A good salad niçoise is a feast for the eyes as well as the palate. Arrange the ingredients with care, either on a large serving dish or individual salad plates.

2 Prick the tuna or swordfish steaks all over with a fork, arrange them in a shallow dish and pour on the marinade, turning the fish to coat each piece. Cover with clear film (plastic wrap) and leave in a cool place for 2–4 hours.

3 Cook the rice in stock or water, following the instructions on the packet, then drain, tip into a bowl and set aside.

4 Make the dressing. Mix the citrus juice, mustard and garlic (if using) in a bowl. Whisk in the oils, then add salt and freshly ground black pepper to taste. Stir 60ml/4 tbsp of the dressing into the rice, then spoon the rice into the centre of a large serving dish.

5 Cook the green beans and broad beans in boiling salted water until tender. Drain, refresh under cold water and drain again. Remove the outer shell from the broad beans and add them to the rice.

6 Discard the outer leaves from the lettuce and tear the inner leaves into pieces. Add to the salad with the tomatoes and coriander. Shell the hard-boiled eggs and cut them into sixths. Preheat the grill (broiler).

7 Arrange the tuna or swordfish steaks on a grill pan. Brush with the marinade and a little extra olive oil. Grill (broil) for 3–4 minutes on each side, until the fish is tender and flakes easily when tested with the tip of a sharp knife. Brush with marinade and more olive oil when turning the fish over.

8 Allow the fish to cool a little, then break the steaks into large pieces. Toss into the salad with the olives and the remaining dressing. Decorate with the eggs and serve.

Energy 685kcal/2874kJ; Protein 41.8g; Carbohydrate 61g, of which sugars 6g; Fat 32.2g, of which saturates 5.7g; Cholesterol 127mg; Calcium 134mg; Fibre 9.2g; Sodium 760mg.

SMOKED TROUT CANNELLONI

ONE OF THE MOST POPULAR PASTA DISHES, CANNELLONI USUALLY HAS A MEAT AND TOMATO FILLING, OR ONE BASED ON SPINACH AND RICOTTA CHEESE. SMOKED TROUT MAKES A DELICIOUS CHANGE.

SERVES FOUR TO SIX

INGREDIENTS

1 large onion, finely chopped
1 garlic clove, crushed
60ml/4 tbsp vegetable stock
2 x 400g/14oz cans chopped
  tomatoes
2.5ml/½ tsp dried mixed herbs
1 smoked trout, about 400g/14oz,
  or 225g/8oz fillets
75g/3oz/½ cup frozen peas, thawed
75g/3oz/1½ cups fresh breadcrumbs
16 no pre-cook cannelloni tubes
salt and ground black pepper

For the sauce
25g/1oz/2 tbsp butter
25g/1oz/¼ cup plain (all-purpose)
  flour
350ml/12fl oz/1½ cups skimmed
  milk
freshly grated nutmeg
25ml/1½ tbsp freshly grated
  Parmesan cheese

1 Put the onion, garlic clove and stock in a large pan. Cover and simmer for 3 minutes. Remove the lid and cook until the stock has reduced entirely.

2 Stir in the tomatoes and dried herbs. Simmer uncovered for 10 minutes, or until the mixture is very thick.

3 Skin the trout with a sharp knife. Flake the flesh, discarding any bones. Put the fish in a bowl and add the tomato mixture, peas and breadcrumbs. Mix well, then season with salt and pepper.

4 Spoon the filling generously into the cannelloni tubes and arrange them in an ovenproof dish. Preheat the oven to 190°C/375°F/Gas 5.

5 Make the sauce. Put the butter, flour and milk into a pan and cook over a medium heat, whisking constantly, until the sauce boils and thickens. Simmer for 2–3 minutes, stirring all the time. Season to taste with salt, freshly ground black pepper and grated nutmeg.

6 Pour the sauce over the stuffed cannelloni and sprinkle with the grated Parmesan cheese. Bake for 30–45 minutes, or until the top is golden and bubbling. Serve immediately.

COOK'S TIP
Smoked trout can be bought as fillets or as whole fish. Look for them in the chiller cabinet of the supermarket.

Energy 367kcal/1548kJ; Protein 24.8g; Carbohydrate 49.7g, of which sugars 11.3g; Fat 9.1g, of which saturates 3.4g; Cholesterol 15mg; Calcium 183mg; Fibre 4g; Sodium 244mg.

STEAMED FISH SKEWERS AND RICE NOODLES

FRESH SUCCULENT FILLETS OF TROUT ARE MARINATED IN A TANGY CITRUS SPICE BLEND, THEN SKEWERED AND STEAMED BEFORE SERVING ON A BED OF FRAGRANT HERB NOODLES.

SERVES FOUR

INGREDIENTS

  4 trout fillets, skinned
  2.5ml/½ tsp turmeric
  15ml/1 tbsp mild curry paste
  juice of 2 lemons
  15ml/1 tbsp sunflower oil
  45ml/3 tbsp chilli-roasted peanuts,
    roughly chopped
  salt and ground black pepper
  chopped fresh mint, to garnish
For the noodles
  300g/11oz rice noodles
  15ml/1 tbsp sunflower oil
  1 red chilli, seeded and finely sliced
  4 spring onions (scallions),
    cut into slivers
  60ml/4 tbsp roughly chopped
    fresh mint
  60ml/4 tbsp roughly chopped fresh
    sweet basil

1 Trim each trout fillet and place in a large bowl. Mix together the turmeric, curry paste, lemon juice and oil, and spoon the mixture over the fish. Season with salt and black pepper, and toss to mix well.

2 For the noodles, place the rice noodles in a bowl and pour over enough boiling water to cover. Leave to soak for 3–4 minutes and then drain. Refresh in cold water, drain and set aside.

COOK'S TIP
Soak the bamboo skewers in water for at least 30 minutes to prevent them from burning during cooking.

3 Thread two bamboo skewers through each trout fillet and arrange in two tiers of a bamboo steamer lined with baking parchment.

4 Cover the steamer and place over a wok of simmering water (making sure the water doesn't touch the bottom of the steamer). Steam the fish skewers for 5–6 minutes, or until the fish is just cooked through.

5 Meanwhile, in a clean wok, heat the oil for the noodles. Add the chilli, spring onions and drained noodles and stir-fry for about 2 minutes and then stir in the chopped herbs. Season with salt and ground black pepper and divide among four bowls or plates.

6 Top each bowl of noodles with a steamed fish skewer and scatter over the chilli-roasted peanuts. Garnish with chopped mint and serve immediately.

Energy 504kcal/2101kJ; Protein 26.5g; Carbohydrate 62.9g, of which sugars 1g; Fat 15.2g, of which saturates 1.7g; Cholesterol 0mg; Calcium 48mg; Fibre 1.4g; Sodium 158mg.

DESSERTS

For those days when you crave a real old-fashioned pudding here are some healthier, but satisfyingly stodgy, alternatives, including fresh, sweet Strawberry Oat Crunch, sophisticated Caramelized Plums with Coconut Rice, and fragrant Indian Rice Pudding. For the ultimate sweet indulgence, try Traditional Halvas, a rich, semolina-based cake.

TRADITIONAL HALVAS

HALVAS TAKES VERY LITTLE TIME TO MAKE AND IT USES STAPLE STORECUPBOARD INGREDIENTS, SUCH AS SEMOLINA AND NUTS. IT MAKES A PERFECT ACCOMPANIMENT TO COFFEE.

SERVES SIX TO EIGHT

INGREDIENTS
500g/1¼lb/2½ cups caster
  (superfine) sugar
1 litre/1¾ pints/4 cups water
1 cinnamon stick
250ml/8fl oz/1 cup olive oil
350g/12oz/2 cups coarse semolina
50g/2oz/½ cup blanched almonds
30ml/2 tbsp pine nuts
5ml/1 tsp ground cinnamon

1 Put the sugar in a heavy pan, pour in the water and add the cinnamon stick. Bring to the boil, stirring until the sugar dissolves, then boil without stirring for about 4 minutes to make a syrup.

2 Meanwhile, heat the oil in a separate, heavy pan. When it is almost smoking, add the semolina gradually and stir constantly until it turns light brown.

3 Lower the heat, add the almonds and pine nuts and brown together for 2–3 minutes, stirring constantly. Take the semolina mixture off the heat and set aside. Remove the cinnamon stick from the hot sugar syrup using a slotted spoon and discard it.

COOK'S TIP
In Greece, this recipe would be made with extra virgin olive oil, but you may prefer the less pronounced flavour of a light olive oil.

4 Protecting your hand with an oven glove or dish towel, carefully add the hot syrup to the semolina mixture, stirring all the time. The mixture will hiss and spit at this point, so stand well away from it.

5 Return the pan to a gentle heat and stir until all the syrup has been absorbed and the mixture looks smooth. Remove the pan from the heat, cover it with a clean dish towel and let it stand for 10 minutes so that any remaining moisture is absorbed.

6 Scrape the mixture into a 20–23cm/ 8–9in round cake tin (pan), preferably fluted, and set it aside. When it is cold, unmould it on to a platter and dust it all over with the ground cinnamon.

COOK'S TIP
Coarse semolina is ground from fine durum wheat. It is usually associated with Indian dishes.

Energy 632kcal/2660kJ; Protein 6.8g; Carbohydrate 99.8g, of which sugars 65.7g; Fat 25.6g, of which saturates 3.1g; Cholesterol 0mg; Calcium 56mg; Fibre 1.5g; Sodium 10mg.

STRAWBERRY OAT CRUNCH

THIS SIMPLE DESSERT LOOKS GOOD AND TASTES DELICIOUS. THE STRAWBERRIES FORM A DELICIOUS FILLING BETWEEN THE LAYERS OF OAT CRUMBLE. ANY LEFTOVERS MAKE A GREAT BREAKFAST TREAT.

SERVES FOUR

INGREDIENTS

150g/5oz/1¼ cups rolled oats
50g/2oz/½ cup wholemeal (wholewheat) flour
75g/3oz/6 tbsp butter
30ml/2 tbsp pear and apple
  concentrate
500g/1¼lb strawberries, hulled
10ml/2 tsp arrowroot
natural (plain) yogurt, custard or
  cream, to serve

VARIATIONS

• Use dried apricots (chop half and cook
the rest to a purée with a little apple
juice) instead of the strawberries.
• Add a few chopped almonds or walnuts
to the crumble mixture.
• Pear and apple concentrate is a highly
concentrated, naturally sweet juice
available from health food stores. Golden
(light corn) syrup or honey can be used.

1 Preheat the oven to 180°C/350°F/
Gas 4. Mix the oats and flour in a bowl.
Melt the butter with the apple and pear
concentrate in a pan; stir into the oats.

2 Purée half the strawberries in
a food processor; chop the rest. Mix the
arrowroot with a little of the strawberry
purée in a small pan, then add the
rest of the purée. Heat gently until
boiling and thickened, then stir in the
chopped strawberries.

3 Spread half the crumble mixture over
the base of a shallow 18cm/7in round
ovenproof dish to form a layer at least
1cm/½in thick. Top the crumble with
the chopped and puréed strawberry
mixture, then add the remaining
crumble mixture, patting it down gently
to form an even layer. Bake the oat
crunch for about 30 minutes, until
golden brown. Serve warm or cold, with
yogurt, custard or cream.

Energy 391kcal/1638kJ; Protein 7.4g; Carbohydrate 50.4g, of which sugars 13.1g; Fat 19.1g, of which saturates 9.8g; Cholesterol 40mg; Calcium 50mg; Fibre 5.1g; Sodium 136mg.

CARAMELIZED PLUMS WITH COCONUT RICE

RED JUICY PLUMS ARE QUICKLY SEARED IN A WOK WITH SUGAR TO MAKE A RICH CARAMEL SAUCE, THEN SERVED WITH STICKY COCONUT-FLAVOURED RICE FOR A SATISFYING DESSERT. THE GLUTINOUS RICE IS AVAILABLE FROM ASIAN STORES, BUT IT HAS TO BE SOAKED OVERNIGHT BEFORE USE.

3 Cover the rice and steam over simmering water for 25–30 minutes, until the rice is tender. (Check the water level and add more if necessary.)

4 Transfer the steamed rice to a wide bowl and set aside for a moment.

5 Combine the coconut cream with the sugar and salt, and pour into a clean wok. Heat gently and bring to the boil, then remove from the heat and pour over the rice. Stir to mix well.

6 Using a sharp knife, cut the plums in half and remove their stones (pits). Sprinkle the sugar over the cut sides.

7 Heat a non-stick wok over a medium-high flame. Working in batches, place the plums in the wok, cut side down, and cook for 1–2 minutes, or until the sugar caramelizes. (You might have to wipe out the wok with kitchen paper in between batches.)

8 Mould the rice into rounds and place on warmed plates, then spoon over the caramelized plums. Alternatively, simply spoon the rice into four warmed bowls and top with the plums.

SERVES FOUR

INGREDIENTS
  6 or 8 firm, ripe plums
  90g/3½ oz/½ cup caster (superfine) sugar
For the rice
  115g/4oz sticky glutinous rice
  150ml/¼ pint/⅔ cup coconut cream
  45ml/3 tbsp caster (superfine) sugar
  a pinch of salt

1 First prepare the rice. Rinse it in several changes of water, then leave to soak overnight in a bowl of cold water.

2 Line a large bamboo steamer with muslin (cheesecloth). Drain the rice and spread out evenly on the muslin.

COOK'S TIP
Sticky glutinous rice does not contain any gluten and is suitable for people with gluten allergies.

Energy 261kcal/1105kJ; Protein 3g; Carbohydrate 62.6g, of which sugars 41.1g; Fat 0.6g, of which saturates 0.1g; Cholesterol 0mg; Calcium 39mg; Fibre 0.7g; Sodium 45mg.

BROWN BREAD ICE CREAM

THE SECRET OF A GOOD BROWN BREAD ICE CREAM IS NOT TO HAVE TOO MANY BREADCRUMBS (WHICH MAKES THE ICE CREAM HEAVY) AND, FOR THE BEST TEXTURE AND DEEP, NUTTY FLAVOUR, TO TOAST THEM UNTIL REALLY CRISP AND WELL BROWNED. SERVE WITH A CHOCOLATE OR FRUIT SAUCE.

SERVES SIX TO EIGHT

INGREDIENTS

115g/4oz/2 cups wholemeal (whole-wheat) breadcrumbs
115g/4oz/½ cup soft brown sugar
2 large (US extra large) eggs, separated
30–45ml/2–3 tbsp Irish Cream liqueur
450ml/¾ pint/scant 2 cups double (heavy) cream

1 Preheat the oven to 190°C/375°F/Gas 5. Spread the breadcrumbs out on a baking sheet and toast them in the oven for about 15 minutes, or until crisp and well browned. Leave to cool.

2 Whisk the sugar and egg yolks together until light and creamy, then beat in the Irish cream liqueur. Whisk the cream until soft peaks form. In a separate bowl, whisk the egg whites until stiff.

COOK'S TIPS
• The Irish cream liqueur can be left out of this delicious ice cream, if preferred, but increase the quantity of double cream or add another favourite liqueur instead.
• When you use alcohol to make ice cream it will slow down the freezing process. To ensure you have enough time, make alcoholic ice creams at least a day before you intend to use them.

3 Sprinkle the breadcrumbs over the beaten egg mixture, add the cream and fold into the mixture with a spoon. Fold in the whisked egg whites. Turn the mixture into a freezerproof container, cover and freeze.

Energy 417kcal/1734kJ; Protein 4.2g; Carbohydrate 28g, of which sugars 17.2g; Fat 32.5g, of which saturates 19.2g; Cholesterol 125mg; Calcium 62mg; Fibre 0.3g; Sodium 143mg.

FRUITY RICE PUDDING CUSTARD

THERE ARE MANY DELICIOUS RICE PUDDINGS, VARYING FROM COUNTRY TO COUNTRY AND EVEN WITHIN REGIONS. RICH-TASTING CREAMED RICE IS WONDERFUL WITH ALL THINGS FTUITY — HERE, SULTANAS AND ZESTY LEMON ARE A WINNING COMBINATION. THE BRANDY OR RUM GIVE A WARMING DEPTH.

SERVES FOUR TO SIX

INGREDIENTS
   60ml/4 tbsp rum or brandy
   75g/3oz/½ cup sultanas (golden
      raisins)
   75g/3oz/scant ½ cup short grain or
      pudding rice
   600ml/1 pint/2½ cups creamy milk
   1 strip pared lemon rind
   ½ cinnamon stick
   115g/4oz/scant ½ cup caster
      (superfine) sugar
   150ml/¼ pint/⅔ cup single (light)
      cream
   2 eggs, plus 1 egg yolk
   almond biscuits, to serve (optional)

1 Warm the rum or brandy in a pan, then pour it over the sultanas. Soak for 3–4 hours or overnight.

2 Cook the rice in boiling water for 10 minutes until slightly softened. Drain.

3 Stir 300ml/½ pint/1¼ cups of milk into the rice in the pan. Add the strip of lemon rind and the cinnamon stick, bring to the boil, then lower the heat and simmer for about 5 minutes.

4 Remove the pan from the heat and stir in half of the sugar. Cover tightly with a damp dish towel held firmly in place with the pan lid. Leave the rice to cool for 1–2 hours.

5 Preheat the oven to 180°C/350°F/ Gas 4. Butter an ovenproof dish (about 1.2 litres/2 pints/5 cups capacity). Sprinkle the sultanas (with any remaining rum or brandy) over the bottom. Stir the rice, which should by now be thick and creamy, most of the liquid having been absorbed, and discard the cinnamon stick and lemon rind. Spoon the rice over the sultanas.

6 Heat the remaining milk with the cream until just boiling. Meanwhile, mix the eggs and egg yolk in a jug. Whisk in the remaining sugar, then the hot milk. Pour the mixture over the rice.

7 Stand the dish in a roasting pan, pour in hot water to come halfway up the sides of the dish and bake for 1–1¼ hours until the top is firm. Serve hot, with almond biscuits, if you like.

COOK'S TIP
This makes a light, creamy rice pudding. If you like your pudding to be denser, cook it for slightly longer.

Energy 326kcal/1366kJ; Protein 8.1g; Carbohydrate 43.7g, of which sugars 33.8g; Fat 11.6g, of which saturates 6.3g; Cholesterol 125mg; Calcium 174mg; Fibre 0.3g; Sodium 79mg.

SWEET FRUITY COUSCOUS

ASIDE FROM ITS SAVOURY ROLE, COUSCOUS IS ALSO EATEN AS A DESSERT OR A NOURISHING BREAKFAST. THIS SWEET, FILLING DISH IS SERVED WITH A DRIED FRUIT COMPOTE, WHICH SHOULD BE PREPARED A COUPLE OF DAYS IN ADVANCE TO ALLOW THE FLAVOURS TO MATURE.

SERVES SIX

INGREDIENTS
  300ml/½ pint/1¼ cups water
  225g/8oz/1⅓ cups medium couscous
  50g/2oz/scant ⅓ cup raisins
  50g/2oz/¼ cup butter
  50g/2oz/¼ cup sugar
  120ml/4fl oz/½ cup milk
  120ml/4fl oz/½ cup double
    (heavy) cream
For the fruit compote
  225g/8oz/2 cups dried apricots
  225g/8oz/1 cup pitted prunes
  115/4oz/¾ cup sultanas (golden
    raisins)
  115g/4oz/1 cup blanched almonds
  175g/6oz/generous ¾ cup sugar
  30ml/2 tbsp rose water
  1 cinnamon stick

1 To make the compote, put the dried fruit and almonds in a bowl and pour in just enough water to cover. Gently stir in the sugar and rose water, and add the cinnamon stick. Cover and leave the fruit and nuts to soak for 48 hours, during which time the water and sugar will form a lovely golden-coloured syrup.

2 To make the couscous, bring the water to the boil in a pan. Stir in the couscous and raisins, and cook gently for 1–2 minutes, until the water has been absorbed. Remove the pan from the heat, cover tightly and leave the couscous to steam for 10–15 minutes.

3 Meanwhile, poach the compote over a gentle heat until warmed through.

4 Tip the couscous into a bowl and separate the grains with your fingertips. Melt the butter and pour it over the couscous. Sprinkle the sugar over the top, then, using your fingertips, rub the butter and sugar into the couscous. Divide the mixture among six bowls.

5 Heat the milk and cream together in a small, heavy pan until just about to boil, then pour the mixture over the couscous. Serve immediately, with the dried fruit compote.

VARIATIONS
• The couscous can be served on its own, drizzled with clear or melted honey instead of with the dried fruit compote.
• The compote is also delicious served chilled on its own or with yogurt.

Energy 708kcal/2974kJ; Protein 10.6g; Carbohydrate 106.6g, of which sugars 86.8g; Fat 29.5g, of which saturates 12.1g; Cholesterol 46mg; Calcium 165mg; Fibre 6.5g; Sodium 87mg.

INDIAN RICE PUDDING

THIS CREAMY RICE PUDDING IS VERY FRAGRANT, BEING SCENTED WITH SAFFRON, CARDAMOM AND FRESHLY GRATED NUTMEG AND HONEY. SHELLED PISTACHIO NUTS GIVE A SUBTLE CONTRAST IN COLOUR AND ADD A DELICIOUS CRUNCH TO THE DESSERT.

SERVES FOUR

INGREDIENTS
  115g/4oz/¾ cup brown short
    grain or pudding rice
  350ml/12fl oz/1½ cups boiling water
  600ml/1 pint/2½ cups semi-
    skimmed (low fat) milk
  6 green cardamom pods, bruised
  2.5ml/½ tsp freshly grated nutmeg
  pinch of saffron threads
  60ml/4 tbsp maize malt syrup
  15ml/1 tbsp clear honey
  chopped pistachio nuts, to decorate

1 Wash the rice under cold running water and place in a pan with the boiling water. Return to the boil and boil, uncovered, for 15 minutes.

2 Pour the milk over the rice, then reduce the heat and simmer, partially covered, for 15 minutes.

3 Add the cardamom pods, grated nutmeg, saffron, maize malt syrup and honey, and cook for a further 15 minutes, or until the rice is tender, stirring occasionally.

4 Spoon the rice into small serving bowls and sprinkle with pistachio nuts before serving hot or cold.

COOK'S TIP
Maize malt syrup is a natural alternative to refined sugar and can be found in health food shops.

Energy 228kcal/961kJ; Protein 7.3g; Carbohydrate 44.7g, of which sugars 21.8g; Fat 2.7g, of which saturates 1.6g; Cholesterol 9mg; Calcium 188mg; Fibre 2.3g; Sodium 106mg.

INDEX

ACKNOWLEDGEMENTS

Recipes: Catherine Atkinson, Pepita Aris, Valerie Barett, Alex Barker, Ghillie Basan, Judy Bastyra, Angela Boggiano, Georgina Campbell, Carole Clements, Trish Davies, Joanna Farrow, Brian Glover, Nicola Graimes, Rosamund Grant, Rebekah Hassan, Shehzad Husain, Christine Ingram, Becky Johnson, Manisha Kanani, Soheila Kimberley, Lucy Knox, Jane Milton, Keith Richardson, Marlena Spieler, Ysanne Spevack, Christopher Trotter, Biddy White Lennon, Kate Whiteman, Carol Wilson, Elizabeth Wolf-Cohen, Jeni Wright.
Home economists: Angela Boggiano, Annabel Ford, Silvano Franco, Kate Jay, Jill Jones, Emma Macintosh, Lucy Mckelvie, Jennie Shapter, Linda Tubby, Suni Vijayakar, Jenny White, Jeni Wright.
Stylists: Shannon Beare, Penny Markham, Marion McLornan, Helen Trent.
Photographers: Frank Adam, David Armstrong, Caroline Barty, Martin Brigdale, Nicki Dowey, Gus Filgate, Amanda Heywood, Ferguson Hill, Janine Hosegood, David Jordan, Clare Lewis, Sara Lewis, William Lingwood, Thomas Odulate, Craig Robertson, Simon Smith.